ISBN- 978-0-578-35376-0

For inquiries: team@thecollegegolfer.com

CONTENTS

INTRODUCTION

There are many ways I could introduce this book to you. I could talk about my life and the many experiences I've had in this game, both good and bad. Or perhaps I could tell stories about college golfers and the great moments we've shared over the years. While that may be interesting, it's not what this book is about. This book is about you, your vision for your future self, and how you're planning to get there.

To that point, I want to ask you two very important questions. First, what are you willing to sacrifice to achieve your vision of the future? Second, what actions are you currently taking to turn your vision into reality? Two very simple questions aimed at the root of success, and it's ok if you can't answer them today, we'll fill in the blanks together.

This book is not a practice manual or detailed review of the golf swing. You won't find anything about the putting stroke or specifications on the latest driver shafts either. No secrets to success or shortcuts to greatness. This book is about a challenging and exciting journey, and how to prepare yourself for the demanding road ahead.

I will ask you difficult questions about who you are, your priorities, commitment and willingness to sacrifice. We will discuss the fundamental building blocks of mental strength and how to cultivate them for yourself, along with strategies to help navigate tough times, on and off the course.

I have spent the majority of my adult life pursuing excellence in competitive golf. My time as a collegiate and professional golfer combined with nearly a decade of college coaching shaped my perspective on this game, and in my eyes, what it takes to be successful. I am offering my perspective to help you focus on what's important, while avoiding common mistakes along the way. More than anything, *I want you to succeed.*

I suppose on a deeper level this book is written to a younger version of myself. I never lacked effort or determination, but I didn't have all the pieces to the mental puzzle. If I was speaking with my younger self I would have tough conversations about discipline, accountability and courage. I would discuss the actions necessary to achieve ambitious goals, and how to prioritize life in a chaotic world. I would explain how these skills transcend the game of golf, unlocking opportunities in all areas of life. If I was speaking with my younger self I'd be direct and to the point, so that's how this book is written. I don't believe in wasting time or sugar coating important information. So with that in mind, I offer you *The College Golfer*.

1 THE REASON

Do you dream of playing college golf in America? Before answering that question, let me describe a scenario that may be of interest to you. In this scenario, you travel the United States playing golf tournaments on the best courses against the best golf teams from across the country. How good is the competition you ask? Simply put, this is the best collection of amateur golf talent in the world, and they're all striving for the same goal; to prove they're the best. These golfers aren't just here for tournament trophies either, they're here preparing for their opportunity to compete at the pinnacle of their sport. For most competitive golfers this is the final step between amateur and professional golf.

Of course, you're not always traveling and playing tournaments in this scenario. Your time between events is spent working with first class golf coaches, professional strength and conditioning specialists, and top professors as you work towards an academic degree. And let's not forget about the world class golf courses, practice facilities, gyms and learning centers you'll have access to, for free. Need some new golf equipment or gear? Well, in this scenario most if not all gear and (golf) supplies are provided at no cost. You may have to pick up the tab for some wedges or a putter, but you have access to discount programs for that too.

Oh, and I mentioned something about a team? That's right, as a member of a collegiate golf team you're surrounded by like minded individuals, collectively working toward common goals. Over time, these individuals may become something more to you. They could become lifelong friends, members of your wedding party, aunts or uncles to your kids, and maybe even family.

The scenario I describe is for the select few willing to sacrifice the traditional college experience for something more. Understand, in this scenario you're competing with the best amateur golfers on the planet, working with demanding coaches *and* maintaining high academic standards. So what's the reward for this demanding scenario? Simply put, you'll have the opportunity to elevate your life higher than you ever thought possible. You see, this scenario was the proving ground for golfers named Jack, Tiger, Annika and Phil. *The best of the best.* So if you think you're strong enough for this scenario, read on. *This is College golf.*

* * *

If you're intrigued with the idea of joining a college golf program, you need to know a few things first. Yes it's true, the collegiate golfer enjoys a uniquely special college experience. But you must earn this experience, and it can be taken away at a moments notice. Before we get into the dynamics of practice, academics and your mental approach, I want you to hear about life as a college golfer away from the course.

First and foremost, being a student athlete is hard. Let that sink in for a moment because there's no getting around it. You are expected to perform on the course and in the classroom at a level consistent with the history and pedigree of your respective school. Make no mistake, your school and coach will hold you to this expectation. When you join a college golf team the university (typically) provides scholarship money, gear, tournament travel and accommodation, world class facilities and (hopefully) great coaching as part of their commitment to you. What do they ask in return? Well, nothing short of an unwavering commitment to the team and your best effort in all school related activities. Hopefully this sounds like a good arrangement because it is, but let's talk about some of the "school related" requirements you'll face as a student athlete.

First, a schedule. That's right, you're now under the direction of a professional coach and he/she will create a schedule that you must adhere to. For example, if the team schedule says 6:00 a.m. workouts Monday/ Wednesday/Friday, that's where you'll be. If the team schedule says 5:30 p.m. study hall Wednesday/Friday, that's where you'll be. If the team schedule says 1:30 p.m. practice Monday through Friday, that's where you'll be. If the team underperforms and coach calls an unscheduled weekend practice, you guessed it, that's where you'll be. So what's my point?

The point is simply this, if you join a college golf program be prepared to sacrifice the majority of your time for the team and coach.

Second, the classwork. Over the years I've received this question more than any from potential recruits, "how much actual school work is required during the semester"? The answer? A lot. You are a full-time student at a major college or university and in the eyes of the school, academics are priority number one. Falling behind on classwork is the primary reason student athletes lose playing privileges during the season. Yes that's right, you can lose playing privileges if you don't maintain the (team) academic standard. Don't worry, we'll cover more on this topic in the "academics" section of the book.

Third, everything else. So you've got a team schedule and plenty of classwork, what else could there be? Well, as a member of the golf team you're also a member of the athletic department. The athletic department consists of all athletic teams and coaches, athletic trainers, support staff and of course the Athletic Director. The Athletic Director oversees the athletic department and periodically calls upon teams to perform tasks for the university. For example, if your school has a football team you may be asked to work a t-shirt stand or sell raffle tickets for the booster club. Or maybe you're asked to work the sidelines during a home soccer or volleyball game collecting wayward shots. What about volunteer work? Absolutely! College athletic teams are called upon by the University to help charitable organizations at various times throughout the year. For example, you could spend a weekend building a home with Habitat for Humanity or work a canned food drive for the United Way. No matter the task, the expectation (and requirement) is your full participation while representing the college and team with integrity. But not to worry, these are great team building activities that provide networking and social opportunities that other students simply aren't afforded.

If the scenario I just described sounds like too much effort and you're unwilling to sacrifice your time, don't. Choose a different path. Being a student athlete is a job and it's not for everyone. But I promise you this, if you commit to the team and everything that goes with it, you'll have a college experience far surpassing that of the normal university student. You will make life-long friends that share your experiences and help develop your character. You will build real world skills like discipline, time management, networking and perseverance. Not to mention, if your long term goal is playing on a professional golf tour, there is no better place to train than a college golf program.

Rest assured, joining a college golf team will be one of the great experiences of your life, but it's not for the faint of heart. Your motivation and commitment to the team must be strong enough to sustain you through late night studying, poor tournament performance, early morning workouts, homesickness, and of course, the demanding coach.

So what's your reason for pursuing this endeavor? Do you have a burning desire to play college or professional golf? If so, you're embarking on a difficult journey, one that very few see to the end. I am here to (humbly) offer my perspective on golf, and life. Hopefully you find inspiration from my experience and this can be a resource for your journey through college and beyond. Above all else, enjoy the process. It's the greatest time of your life!

2 MINDSET

In short, I believe developing both the mind and body are equally important to the competitive golfer. If your goal is becoming an elite player you must train your mind like you train your body. So what does that look like? Well, if you're like me you've spent countless hours on the course, driving range, putting green and short game area honing your physical skills. Not to mention the gym work that's been a staple of my routine for the past twenty-five years. Of course, there's a mental aspect included in all this physical training, but unlocking your full potential requires a much deeper look inside your psyche.

For example, my mental approach to golf (and life) developed from many hours studying sport psychologists, competitive golfers, military leaders, motivational speakers, successful entrepreneurs and of course, friends and family. For me, their combined perspective led to an obvious conclusion; highly successful people master and utilize key mental characteristics, leading to favorable outcomes regardless of their profession. However, before we unpack each of these mental characteristics, let's focus for a moment on the primary attribute that binds all high-achievers together - *the mastering of their attention.*

You may have heard or read about popular golf specific attention protocols like "broad external" for assessing your environment, or "narrow external" for engaging a target during your pre-shot routine. These are important concepts and worth understanding, but not what I'm speaking about at the moment. I'm asking you to take a much broader look at your life, and evaluate where your attention goes day to day, week to week. In a world that's become incredibly chaotic and noisy, where you place your attention is of utmost importance.

Attention can be thought of as the direction of your thoughts at any given moment, and focus refers to the amount of concentration you apply to those thoughts over time. Think of daydreaming versus concentrated effort. You could be daydreaming or casually thinking about the subject of your next term paper, versus concentrating on it and actually writing it. Same subject, different amount of focus.

Now that we've defined the terms, consider deep diving into your daily routines and habits to identify where your attention is throughout the day. How much of your attention are you "giving away" to things that don't contribute to success? Start with obvious areas like phone usage, video games, television and social media. Keep in mind, the average teenager in the United States averaged roughly 7.5 hours a day on their phone in 2022. I'm not suggesting that's entirely negative, but I'm guessing a large percentage of that time could be trimmed off in pursuit of a goal. And that's the most important aspect of reclaiming your attention, *you need to recognize what you're giving up by not managing your attention effectively.*

Consider the following scenario with two competitive golfers in the same age bracket; we'll call them Player A and Player B. Both players balance their time between academics and other non-golf obligations evenly. However, player A allocates five hours a day to social media, while Player B stays clear of such platforms altogether. Instead of scrolling instagram or watching YouTube videos, Player B devotes his attention towards refining his goals and objectives. He visualizes the journey ahead, creates and executes detailed practice plans and religiously adheres to a fitness protocol. Player B isn't consumed with other people's lives and does not fear missing out on anything. Simply put, Player B is on a **mission**. Now, it's possible Player A does some of these same things, but it's highly unlikely that the quantity and quality of attention is equal to Player B. There simply isn't enough time in the day. In this scenario, who's likely to ascend faster?

Consider this perspective, your attention at any given moment is inherently linked to time. Time is a tricky concept because we all perceive it differently. In my twenties, I felt like time was an infinite resource, and admittedly, I squandered some of it. Now, in my forties, I see time through a different lens. It's much more valuable to me now, and as a result, I'm acutely aware of my daily behaviors. The truth is, time is a finite resource and the focus of our attention ultimately shapes who and what we'll become in this world. At this stage of my life I'm no longer willing to donate large sums of my attention to big tech companies or social media platforms. Spending time with my family, pursuing fitness and health goals and undertaking projects like authoring this book are far more important. So I'll ask you this question: what do you want to achieve in your lifetime? What are your grand ambitions? If you're striving for greatness, you'll need to harness your attention and maintain laser sharp focus.

The following five chapters are dedicated to the mental characteristics necessary to play elite level golf. Make no mistake, building mental acuity is a lifelong endeavor. I can offer the building blocks but you must do the work. Over the past decade working with collegiate golfers I have identified five mental traits necessary for success on the course, and in life. Those traits include discipline, accountability, the management of expectations, perseverance and confidence. This is a challenging endeavor and precisely why we'll continue the discussion on mindset training with the most foundational element of all; *discipline*. Because without it, **you are lost**.

- Chapter Summary -

1. Developing the mind and body are equally important to the competitive golfer.

2. All high-achievers manage their attention effectively.

3. If you have grand ambitions you'll need to harness your attention and maintain laser sharp focus.

4. The five mental attributes all successful people master are: discipline, accountability, the management of expectations, perseverance and self-confidence.

3 DISCIPLINE

Let me offer you a couple sobering statistics from information gathered in 2020. According to the National High School Golf Association in the United States, of the roughly two-hundred thousand high school golfers in America (men's and women's), only 3% reach NCAA division 1 golf programs. Taking that a step further, only 1 in 16,486 (.006%) male golfers achieve full time status on the PGA Tour. For you ladies out there, the odds of reaching the LPGA Tour aren't much better. Of course, there are other options for playing college and professional golf, but if you aspire to play at the highest level of either, the odds are not in your favor. So the question is, how will *you* reach your goal of playing high level college or professional golf? Are you uniquely talented? Do you have an unstoppable work ethic? Will you sacrifice *everything* to achieve your goals?

This is the cost of becoming an elite college and professional golfer, and discipline is the currency.

So, what is discipline? Discipline is the fundamental characteristic shared by most, if not all successful people. Discipline goes to war with excuses, bad weather, sore muscles, fatigue and mental weakness. Discipline picks you up when you're down, and humbles you when you're up. Discipline is the voice in your head telling you to hit the extra range balls, finish the putting drill, complete the final set in the gym and finish assignments on time. Discipline is taking the hard road, making sacrifices and being accountable for all aspects of your life. Discipline is the foundation for mental strength, you simply need to commit to its path.

At its core, discipline is a combination of three key attributes; clear and precise goals, great decision making and willingness to sacrifice. *Highly successful people are masters of these attributes.*

Discipline is very difficult to maintain without a clear, precise direction. So what are your goals? What do you want to become and how are you going to get there? *Writing down your goals and creating an action plan sets you on the path to discipline.* Start by writing out crystal clear descriptions of what you want in each area of your life (golf, health, relationships, etc), and be specific, this is your life we're talking about. If you don't know what you want for certain areas of your life, that's ok. Start with the areas you're clear about and go from there. Once you've created your vision(s), start building action plans for each respective area. You don't need a perfect plan when you start, simply write down the actions you believe necessary to achieve your goals. Your plan will evolve and improve over time, but you must start with something. Committing to a plan (regardless of how good it is) dramatically increases your chances of success because it gives you direction, identifies priorities and cuts out unnecessary noise. *I cannot stress this point enough.* Highly successful people create and execute plans with ruthless efficiency. This is a skill you must develop.

Writing down your goals and creating a plan is a must, but it's not enough. *You must actively decide to engage in your plan each and every day.* Think about it like this, your life can be summed up as a series of decisions and your success (or failure) depends on the quality of your decision making. *Decisions lead to actions, and the actions you choose today define who you'll be tomorrow.* Don't let anyone fool you, every decision matters. How you choose to interact with others, every meal, every practice, every workout, *it all matters.* Remember this, there are consequences (good and bad) to every action you take. The severity of the consequence depends on the action itself, but all actions affect our ability to achieve success. Actions cause a ripple effect bringing us closer to our goals, or pushing us farther away. The most disciplined people (almost) always make decisions that bring them closer to achieving their goals. I say almost because no one is perfect and even highly disciplined people make poor decisions. But when they *do* make a poor decision, they immediately adjust and get back on their path. This type of decision making can be very difficult, especially for young people considering different possibilities for their lives and the best direction(s) to pursue. But here's the challenge, our world is highly competitive and ascending to the top of any sport or profession requires great decision making from an early age. Competitive golf is no different and I'd argue it's one of the most demanding fields in the world. Whether it's a top amateur, collegiate or professional event, you're competing with a global talent pool and there's a finite amount of positions available for each event. Additionally, as you move through your golf career the rewards for good play continue improving (money, sponsorships, tournament exemptions, etc.), so you'll be competing with some of the most talented, motivated humans on the planet. In my experience, the majority of these people are very disciplined decision makers.

So what does it take to become a great decision maker? *Nothing short of an unrelenting ability to make sacrifices.* The word "decision" is derived from the Latin word decidere, which literally means "to cut off". In other words, once you make a decision *all* other possibilities are "cut off". To that point, the act of sacrificing means we choose one thing over another, and in doing so, miss the experience of whatever we chose not to do. It's a simple concept, but one that can be incredibly complex for young people. For example, let's say you decide to practice on a Saturday afternoon instead of hanging out with friends at a football game. There is real emotion tied into that decision because you *want* to spend time with your friends. You may also want to practice but the fear of missing out on experiences with friends is a powerful motivator. In college you'll face countless opportunities to engage in experiences that may not align with your goals. Don't get me wrong, these experiences aren't necessarily bad for you either, quite the opposite actually. I'm talking about normal campus activities like social gatherings, sports events, dating, and everything else the majority of college students engage in. These are great opportunities to meet new people, and yes, there will be time for you to enjoy *some* of these activities. However, I want you to get familiar with the concept of delayed gratification; *sacrificing immediate satisfaction for a better long term outcome*. The question you must ask yourself is simple; what am I willing to sacrifice to achieve my goals? Your answer to this question is immeasurably important, and in my opinion, the #1 predictor of your ability to achieve a goal.

Remember, there are countless "great" golfers in the world. To become truly "elite", you must be willing to sacrifice more than your competition. Understandably, this may sound harsh and you could be asking yourself, "what's wrong with being great?". Well, there's nothing wrong with being great but I'm coming to you with a different perspective. I've coached *many* great golfers who aspired to play professional golf after college. Of those golfers, all but a handful are now working in careers outside competitive golf. This is the reality for 99% of college golfers, and that's ok. But I think most, if not all of these former student athletes would tell you that (more) disciplined decision making during high school and college would have greatly improved their chances of a career in professional golf. Your coach can help you understand this concept but it's up to you to make sacrifices when no one else is around. It's a simple choice, you either take actions bringing you closer to your goals, or you don't. I want you to think about this concept when you are considering what to focus your attention on. After all, focusing on your goals and making decisions toward achieving them is a core principle of sacrifice. If you want to join the tiny percentage of people that become elite college or professional golfers, you must be willing to sacrifice what others will not.

* * *

When you join a college golf program you'll be asked to set goals and discuss your plan of action with your coach. Of course, these conversations occur between coaches and athletes in every sport, worldwide. It's during these conversations that coaches ask players if they're willing to make sacrifices, commit to the team and do everything in their power to achieve success. These are not only conversations, they're agreements between the player and coach. When you tell a coach you're willing to do "whatever it takes" to win, that becomes the expectation. Now the coach expects you to be the first person at practice, and the last to leave. It means you're up to date on school work so you're always available to play. Oh and you better give 100% at team workouts, because that's part of winning too. But what happens when you fall below the standard you set for *yourself*? What happens when you start making excuses for your actions? Let's be honest, no one *wants* to be the person making excuses, so why does it happen so often? The answer is lack of discipline and accountability. Making excuses is a protective mechanism against humiliation and embarrassment. *We all do it.* Fortunately, you don't have to accept this as your default reaction to failure. Trust me, you won't feel good about yourself making excuses and blaming everything, and everyone for your mistakes.

Discipline and accountability are the most important subjects I discuss with players and the conversations go something like this; the player may say "coach, my short game stinks and I can't putt." Or, "Coach, I need to drop my english class because the teacher doesn't like me." Or, "coach, I can't make 6AM workouts because I'm not sleeping enough at night." Regardless of the issue, the solution is always the same.

First, you must understand that by telling yourself you "can't" do something, you're right, you can't. Instead, you replace "can't" with "can", and start the process from there. It is amazing how you can affect change by simply improving your self talk and applying a positive attitude to the situation. This fundamental shift in self talk is essential for accountability, and yes, it requires discipline to apply it to all situations in life. More on self talk later.

Second, I always ask the player if they've done everything in their power to achieve success in the given area. Let's examine the player struggling on the greens. Does the player have a positive mindset? Has he checked his fundamentals (alignment, ball position, posture, etc.)? Is the player implementing putting drills and researching new ideas to improve? Does the player spend extra time on the putting green after practice? Is the player asking coaches and teammates for help? Or, is the player frustrated and simply making excuses because it's the easy way out? More often than not, the player admits he hasn't done *everything* in his power to achieve success. Admitting to yourself that you haven't done everything in your power to achieve success *should* be a lightbulb moment. The moment when the player begins to understand the mindset of the disciplined athlete. When your mind offers you an excuse or the easy way out of a situation, you must say *no*. You will not make the excuse, you will not accept failure, and you most certainly will not show weakness... to *yourself*.

It is critical to understand and identify when your mind tries to fool you into taking the easy path because it happens all the time, to everyone. You *must not* take the easy path. Next time your mind offers you an excuse, simply acknowledge it, then proceed with the opposite action. Apply this mentality to all situations because this is the mentality that wins on the course, in the gym, in the classroom and most importantly, in life.

We all use tools and practice aids to help our swing mechanics but one of the best mental tools you can own is a mirror, and no, not for checking your set-up or takeaway. I'm talking about the mirror you keep in the privacy of your bedroom or bathroom. When you face a mirror and ask the question "have I done *everything* in my power to achieve success in this area?", you're only talking to one person and it's the one person you cannot lie to, yourself.

Only the strongest, most disciplined

minds use the mirror because most cannot handle the truth. The truth that you're not doing everything in your power to succeed. Most people will simply make excuses instead of identifying weakness and attacking it. These people will not become professional golfers, and most won't have successful college careers either. However, if you face the mirror and embrace discipline you can achieve success like you never thought possible. Please understand, you have *never* done enough. The practice, workouts, mental training and sacrifice continue on for a lifetime (regardless of your chosen profession). You *must* make the sacrifices others are unwilling to make. Stay the extra hour at practice, finish the assignment to the best of your ability, skip the late night parties, embrace early morning workouts, eat quality food and prioritize sleep. Be the player standing alone on a cold evening finishing your drills knowing you're one step closer to your ultimate goal. Because the truth is, *you are already running out of time.* If your goal is competing with the best, you need to recognize who you're competing against; the select few willing to sacrifice *everything* for their one shot at greatness. If you expect to compete on this level, *you must be this person.* The person inspiring others to be great. The person making sacrifices. The person taking on the challenge alone. *That is Discipline.*

-Chapter Summary-

1. Discipline is comprised of three key elements: clear and precise goals, great decision making and a willingness to sacrifice.

2. Writing down your goals and creating an action plan sets you on the path to discipline.

3. You must actively decide to engage in your plan each and every day.

4. The actions you choose today define who you'll become tomorrow.

5. Great decision makers have an unrelenting ability to make sacrifices.

6. If you expect greatness, you must be willing to make the sacrifices other will not.

4 ACCOUNTABILITY

We just spoke about discipline and why I believe it's the most important mental attribute for the competitive golfer. Now I'd like to introduce discipline's best friend and most trusted advisor, *accountability*. By definition, accountability is "being liable'" for something. For example, as a college golf coach I was accountable for everything in relation to the men's golf program including academic advising and performance, travel, team practice and workouts, recruiting, extra curricular programming and of course, tournament performance. As the leader of the program I accepted full responsibility for everything on this list, and any (team or individual) shortcomings throughout the season fell directly on my shoulders. As a coach, I *owned* this responsibility. If the team failed on any level, I looked no further than myself for blame. So now it's your turn to embrace accountability, and pay close attention to the next few words because they could change your life forever (they did for me).

There is a person out there depending on you to make the right decisions today. In fact, that person is BEGGING you to make the right decisions today. *That person is your future self.* Ultimately, your future self's success is 100% dependent on your ability to make great decisions today. Your future self (humbly) requests you do everything in your power *today,* to become great tomorrow. Believe me, your future self understands the sacrifices necessary for success. Don't we all wish we could go back a few years and ask ourselves to work a little harder? Sacrifice a little more? *Do* a little more?

Ask yourself this, do you want to be a great college golfer? Do you want a long career on a professional golf tour? Do you want to push yourself and sacrifice everything to achieve your goals? Do you want *success*? If the answer is yes then you must hold yourself accountable for all aspects of your life. This isn't just about being disciplined, it's the combination of discipline and accountability that unlocks your full potential. For example, many college golfers are disciplined enough to work hard at practice and team workouts. Many students go to class, finish homework assignments and achieve good grades. Many people go to work, raise families and live productive lives. And make no mistake, that's admirable. That's disciplined. That's a respectable way to live. But how many of those people aspired for more? How many intended to play professional golf or fulfill a childhood dream? How many wish they could go back and work a little harder, be more disciplined, hold themselves accountable? *How many fell short of their dreams?*

So when my players tell me they want to play professional golf it means they aspire to the highest (.006%) of all male golfers on the planet. And whether they know it or not, it also means they'll have to be among the most disciplined, self-accountable athletes in the world.

In my experience, the combination of discipline and accountability creates the most powerful force available to man; *purposeful action*. When actions are infused with purpose you can achieve extraordinary feats. Purpose is developed through intense self scrutiny, you must understand this. Look yourself in the mirror, ask the hard questions and answer them honestly. Did you attack your weaknesses today? Did you finish the assignment to the *best* of your ability? Did you give amazing effort at practice? Or, did you simply show up and go through the motions, failing to achieve the standard you've set for yourself? If you failed to achieve the standard you've set for yourself I want you to feel that emotion. I want you to feel that frustration. I want you to feel that anger. Because that's the fuel you need. That's your future self asking you to work harder, do more, *be more.*

It's not enough to simply show up and do the work. It's critical to stay present in each moment, always aware and working toward your ultimate goal. In real time you must identify when you're feeling weak and looking for shortcuts. At some point everyone hears their inner voice saying "we've done enough for today". Or "we can easily get this done tomorrow". Override that voice when you hear it, because that voice isn't holding you accountable. That voice seeks comfort. That voice wants the easy way out. That voice is *weak*. But the more you override that voice the more powerful you become. As you build mental strength you'll handle discomfort and suffering with ease and you'll change your inner voice. Instead of seeking comfort, safety and procrastination, your inner voice pushes you harder and farther than ever before. You will come to understand that accountability, discipline and mental strength are forged from suffering and discomfort.

But beware, that weak inner voice never goes away. You can silence it, file it away and overcome it for long stretches of time. But the moment you give in, the moment you think you've done enough the voice returns. Asking if you've had enough. Asking if you're ready to quit. You will fight against weakness the rest of your life. But it's a fight you can, and *must* win.

* * *

Have you ever participated on a team? Have you bonded with people through shared experiences of hardship, struggle, sacrifice, victory and defeat? There's something uniquely satisfying about coming together as a group, developing team chemistry, working together and achieving goals. If you've been involved with a situation like this you understand what I'm saying. And since you're joining a college golf team (or already on one), it's a good time to discuss how personal accountability interacts with team culture, and how to be a great teammate.

Great teams typically have great leadership, either from coaches, players or a combination of both. Without great leadership teams are simply a collection of people with individual goals, rarely achieving team success. Great leaders hold themselves accountable for everything, never blaming others while prioritizing the team above all else. So how does that affect you? Quite simply, this is your opportunity to become a *leader*.

When I played college golf I had the honor of serving as team co-captain for two years. I didn't ask for the position, my teammates voted me in. They voted me in (presumably) because in their eyes I exemplified what it meant to be a leader. I brought great effort to practice and workouts, excelled academically, helped teammates develop skills (on and off the course), and performed well in competition. As an older player on the team I understood my role; my teammates counted on me to lead by example because I had experience and life skills. As leaders of the team my co-captain and I spoke often about setting the right example, holding teammates accountable and teaching younger players how to lead. This experience helped me transition from player to coach, and continues helping me today.

So how do you become a great teammate and leader of your team? Well, it doesn't happen overnight and the first step to becoming a leader is becoming a great teammate. Great teammates are committed to the team process which means showing up to workouts, class, practice and team functions with a positive attitude, ready to work. It means providing an example for your teammates regardless of your position or stature on the team. It means being accountable for all aspects of life on campus including academics. It means coaches can depend on you to make great decisions, day after day for the greater good of the team. By owning your personal responsibilities and committing to the team, you become a great teammate. This is the first requirement of leadership.

As you continue maintaining high standards your teammates take notice. They notice you excelling on the course. They notice you excelling in the classroom and getting stronger in the gym. They notice coaches looking to you for input on team related matters. Not only will they see you as a great teammate, they will *respect* you for your consistent effort. Respect from your teammates is the ultimate compliment and once you have their respect, you can *lead* them. But there's one more aspect of leadership that must be developed first. *Humility.*

Being a great teammate and leader requires humility. Humility is understanding you're not bigger than the team, you're *part* of the team. Great teams are comprised of people sacrificing personal benefit for the greater good of the team. They understand the team is more important than the individual, and personal advancement is done through team success. Great leaders put their personal agenda on hold to help teammates. This is a sacrifice all leaders make. When you show your teammates you're willing to sacrifice your agenda to help with theirs, they will see you differently. They will admire you, they will respect you, and they will *follow* your lead. This type of leadership creates an environment where teammates look to help one another, and when teammates help one another learning occurs exponentially. One teammate's strength is employed to help another's weakness and so on. Great teammates hold each other accountable and support each other through difficult times. This creates a bond, inspiring individuals to work for each other and toward common team goals.

When speaking about humility we must address ego and how it plays an important role in your development. Simply put, your ego is how you separate from other individuals and create an identity for yourself. There's nothing inherently wrong with having a strong ego, self-belief and confidence are required to achieve difficult goals. However, you must keep your ego in check and remain humble because ego can be the enemy of accountability. In other words, the moment you think you've done enough to be successful your ego has won. An overinflated ego would have you believe you're the best and you don't have to continue learning or pay attention to details. Your ego certainly doesn't want you looking in the mirror, identifying weaknesses and admitting you could do better. Rather, egocentric people look in the mirror to *admire* themselves. This mentality is poisonous. This mentality leads to complacency, overconfidence and *arrogance.* Arrogant people put themselves first, always. They don't look to help others, they look for personal gain above all else. This mentality is cancerous for a team. When individuals prioritize personal gain over team success, the collective group turns on itself. No longer do you have an atmosphere of growth, support and camaraderie. You have individuals unwilling to share their expertise for fear their teammates will pass them by. This "fear" consumes individuals to the point they are unwilling to share anything. The team is *finished.*

So keep your ego in check, be accountable, self-evaluate, and always look for ways to help and support the team. As a leader you will sacrifice your time and energy, but in return you'll feel a sense of purpose and self worth you've never felt before.

-Chapter Summary-

1. Your future self's success is 100% dependent on your ability to make great decisions today.

2. The combination of discipline and accountability create purposeful action.

3. Accountability starts with intense self-evaluation.

4. The initial phase of leadership is being a great teammate and leading by example.

5. Being a great leader requires humility; you're not bigger than the team, you're part of it.

6. An unchecked ego leads to self-admiration and arrogance.

5 EXPECTATIONS

I believe discipline and accountability are the two most important attributes for the competitive golfer. The next step is blending discipline and accountability with realistic expectations, because faulty expectations can derail even the most committed golfers. By definition, an expectation is a belief that something will happen or be the case in the future. Expectations determine your perspective on everything in life, and therefore, your emotional response to it. As you well know, emotion plays a huge role in the success, or failure of a golfer.

First things first, you must understand, and more importantly, *accept* that unfortunate events and adversity exist on the golf course. Admittedly, we all have rounds where everything falls into place and the game seems effortless. Unfortunately, adversity lurks around every corner on a golf course, and you'll face it eventually. There are simply too many variables outside our control that (randomly) change throughout the round. Like it or not adversity is coming, and your response to it directly impacts your success as a competitive golfer.

Most competitive golfers know that emotional control is critical to their success. So why do golfers (especially good ones) get so mad on the course? The answer is simple, *unrealistic* expectations. Now look, I've had my fair share of blow-ups on the golf course. We've all hit great shots that smash into unseen sprinkler heads, then fly into a water hazard causing a triple-bogey. Or the perfect drive that somehow clips the cart path and goes out of bounds. *Of course* these situations are frustrating and you're allowed to have a (natural) emotional response. But be careful, if that emotional response lingers into something more, you've probably got unrealistic expectations about golf, and maybe life too.

Let me ask you a question, do you feel *entitled* to a great result if you execute a perfect golf shot? You better think long and hard about this because this is key to understanding expectations and controlling your emotions on the course. Let me explain.

You should absolutely *believe* in your ability to execute a great golf shot. But don't mistake believing in your ability with being entitled to a great result. Entitlement is the cause of most anger and frustration on the golf course. For example, do you get upset with a bad bounce or a bird chirping in your backswing? Do you throw a club if the wind blows your shot off-course? Do you lose your mind if your putt hits a pitch-mark on the green and lips out? I don't know about you specifically, but I've witnessed enough (emotional) meltdowns on the golf course to know the answer to these questions is typically, *yes.*

Let me offer you a suggestion regarding your expectations. Stop worrying about things you cannot control and put every ounce of energy into what you *can* control. And yes, you should have incredibly high expectations for everything within your control. Preparing for a tournament, studying for an exam, eating quality foods are all examples of variables within your control. *Dominate them.*

While we're on the subject of

tournament and exam preparation, ask yourself this, how do you prepare for these events in your life? If you don't have a system in place, I suggest you develop one tailored to your skill set. Let's examine tournament prep for a moment. The following is the (basic) protocol I use to ensure both mental and physical readiness leading into an event.

First, I *consciously* commit my time and energy to the event. In other words, the event is priority number one and all non-essential life activities are sacrificed. Therefore, during the prep phase my time and energy are committed to practice, exercise, sleep, nutrition and mental health (and homework during my college years). These variables are within my control and optimizing each one is my *job*. My success in the event is directly correlated with my commitment and effort in each of these areas.

Second, I write down two mental cues that go with me every time I'm on the course, either practicing or playing. Number one; *when I'm on the course I will do everything in my power to execute a perfect pre-shot routine, committing 100% to each shot.* Simple. Number two; *the moment I strike the shot I accept the result and move forward, no exceptions.* You see, I *expect* to perform a perfect pre-shot routine. I *expect* to accept the result no matter how "unlucky" it may be. I expect to do these two things because they are within my control, and nothing else matters. I write these mental cues down so I never forget them, it's that important.

By owning this philosophy about expectations I rarely get upset with outcomes out of my control. Of course, this perspective comes with age (and many bad reactions on the golf course), but it's critical you understand and adopt this philosophy as soon as possible. Remember, the golf course doesn't owe you anything, and neither does life for that matter. If you expect success you must earn it, and the formula is consistent effort, mental fortitude and perseverance. If you continually get upset over uncontrollable events in your life, you will *not* fulfill your potential. So don't complain when your ball hits a tree and goes out of bounds. Don't complain when you hit a ball-mark, missing the three-foot putt. Don't complain when your approach shot takes a hard bounce over the green. Because the harsh reality is, no one cares about your bad break. People only care about *how you react* to the bad break. Did you crumble, or did you fight on? You should *expect* to work hard on every shot, every round, for the rest of your life.

* * *

If someone asked you to describe yourself as a golfer, what would you say? Do you see yourself as a player capable of shooting under par consistently? Or maybe you're more of a mid-seventies golfer who occasionally breaks par? It's important to identify exactly how you feel about yourself as a golfer, *then let it go forever.* That's right, better read that again. Identify how you see yourself as a golfer (in relation to score), then forget it. This is an exercise I do with players revealing a key psychological boundary most competitive golfers eventually face.

For example, at the beginning of each semester I'd ask my players to outline their short and long-term goals. I usually got responses like "I want to improve my short game", or "I want to hit more greens in regulation". All the normal things golfers think about. But occasionally I got this, "I want to improve my scoring average from 74 to 72". Ok, that seems fair enough, right? Well, there's nothing wrong with striving for a better scoring average, but there's a fatal flaw in this thinking. You see, the player averaging 74 may very well be capable of averaging 70. But this player's self-image (or insecurity) only allows him to verbalize a goal that seems attainable or reasonable. Why? Perhaps this player lacks self confidence, or maybe he doesn't want to sound arrogant by declaring his mission to average 66. Who knows. The point is, don't box yourself into a scoring average that seems appropriate for you.

There's a phenomenon in sports psychology describing this very thing. Players associating themselves with a particular score (usually) find their way back to, or within 1-2 shots of that score during most rounds. For example, have you ever started a round with three or four birdies in a row? If so, what happened? Did you break the course record? Did you shoot your personal best score? Or, did you get nervous and make several bogey's down the stretch to shoot closer to your scoring average? I bet most of you said the latter, and you're not alone. Your brain is very clever, and if you decide consciously that you're a person that shoots 75, you can expect a whole bunch of 75's (assuming you're good enough to shoot 75). Whether your playing above or below your capability, your subconscious attempts to get you back to your *expected* score.

Here's what I suggest, stop thinking about your (golf) self-image as a score. Instead, think of yourself as the person who works tirelessly knowing that your scores will continually improve as you build more consistent skills. You're not playing golf to achieve a particular score. Instead, your goal is executing a perfect process shot after shot, to achieve the best possible score for each round. Then, when you're on the course you simply execute a perfect pre-shot routine, accept the result and move on to the next shot. Never thinking about what's ahead of, or behind you, just the current shot. If you're playing well and feeling nervous simply remind yourself this is what you prepared for. The long hours are paying off and shooting lower scores is part of the plan. Stay present, stay focused, lock into your process and enjoy the ride. You'll add up the scores later.

-Chapter Summary-

1. Faulty expectations can derail the most talented, committed golfers.

2. The most important aspect of managing expectations is learning to accept outcomes.

3. Entitlement is the cause of most anger and frustration on the golf course.

4. Utilize your energy on the golf course for controlling the variables you can control, and let everything else go.

5. During tournament preparation, commit 100% of your time and energy to the variables that support great play, on and off the course.

6. Forget about seeing yourself as a golfer that shoots a particular score. Instead, become a golfer who's 100% focused on the process.

6 PERSEVERANCE

I am fortunate to have competed against and worked with many great players over the course of my career. I have coached collegiate golfers from 10 countries spanning three continents. I have worked with professional golfers, juniors, seniors, weekend warriors and everything in between. What I've come to realize is no matter the skill level, true competitors share a common trait; *perseverance*. In short, perseverance is the ability to stay on course and overcome something difficult. Sounds simple enough, right?

Several years back I coached a very good player who did everything right. He held himself accountable, was a disciplined worker and sacrificed for the team. He studied the game and understood course management as well as any college player I've coached. He was excelling both on, and off the course.

During our fall season we were

competing in a conference event and following the first round, this player was challenging for the lead. He was positive, aggressive and playing well. If you're familiar with college golf tournaments you know that coaches typically see their players every 5-6 holes during a round (unless they're walking with one particular player). Well, following the initial 18 holes (we typically play 36 the first day), each time I saw this player he was becoming more and more frustrated. Even though he was only a couple shots off the lead, he was complaining about the course, the greens and various other bad breaks. This was the first time I'd seen him in this condition. I caught up with him on his second to last hole of the day and he was clearly distraught. He was moving slowly, head down, *defeated.* He approached me and said "coach, no matter what I do I can't make a putt. I'm going through a perfect pre-shot, using perfect aim-point, making a perfect stroke, and it simply won't go in". This (usually) confident, capable golfer, was broken. In fact, he was nearly in tears. The following day we completed the event, and even though it was in the past, the player still lamented his "misfortune" on the greens the previous day. His poor putting continued throughout the final round, although he did manage a top 10 finish. However, in his view something was very wrong. You see, this player believed whole heartedly that if he did everything right, he *deserved* a quality result. At the time, he wasn't equipped mentally to overcome repeated "misfortune". He couldn't persevere. Over time this player and I worked on expectations and accepting (shot) results, which led to a much improved mental approach.

Most golfers face scenarios like this at some point in their college career. Unfortunately, it's not just the golf course challenging the collegiate golfer. Academic stress, fear of missing out on social events, team competition (and many other things) are all challenges you may face. So how will you handle adversity when it's presented to you?

Teaching perseverance is tricky, some people inherently have it, some don't. As a coach it's my job to prepare players for adversity. Describing what it looks like, how you'll feel when it happens, and ultimately, how to deal with it. But some people simply won't persevere. They wither in the face of adversity, turning away from any and all challenges. This *cannot* be you. As a collegiate golfer you *will* face challenges. You must face them head on, and your reaction to those challenges shapes your future as a golfer, and as an individual in this world.

So how will you react when you bogey the first four holes in a big event? What happens when you have major homework assignments due in multiple classes at the same time? How will you react if you don't make the travel team for the first three events? These are real challenges college golfers face, and in some cases, cause players to disengage from the team and sometimes even quit altogether. If you don't know how to face adversity, that's ok, you can learn.

First, when adversity strikes you must do your best to accept the situation for what it is, *as soon as possible*. The sooner you accept your new reality, the sooner you can start looking for a solution. Second, focus *all* your attention and energy on what you *can* control. For example, lets say you don't make the travel team for the first event of the season. This can be incredibly frustrating because competing and sharing the tournament experience with teammates is why you're there. Missing events was not part of your plan. But the reality is, only 5 players travel to events (typically), so that leaves the other 5 players at home. So what can you control in this scenario? How will you make the best of this situation? Start by accepting that you didn't play well enough to qualify for the travel team. No excuses, no blame. Reframe this experience as a positive, an opportunity to get ahead while the team is on the road. Next, evaluate your game and create a practice plan to attack your weaknesses (more on this later). Then take time to catch up on homework, work with your strength coach, get help from professors, get quality sleep and eat nutritious foods. *Lead* yourself towards a favorable outcome in the future. I know this strategy sounds easy enough, but there's an alternative path college golfers take when facing this scenario. Unfortunately, some players don't see missing an event as an opportunity to improve. They sulk, they get frustrated and disengage from the process. They start looking for other things to do while the team is on the road. Maybe they skip a workout or homework assignment. Maybe they attend parties over the weekend, falling behind on rest and eating poorly. This player is turning away from adversity, avoiding the challenge altogether. This is a very *dangerous* habit.

When you seek the path of least resistance you're training your mind to avoid adversity. At it's worst, this becomes your default mode and small challenges become insurmountable. For this person, the reaction to a tough situation like bogeying the first 4 holes of an event is simply giving up and blaming someone or something for the bad result. Or how about the difficult homework assignment? I've seen athletes fake illness, cheat, lie and make incredible excuses to avoid doing the work. What about team workouts? Same story. The athlete can't sleep, has an injury or too much fatigue to exercise. Anything to avoid the work. This mentality is poisonous and can infect every aspect of your life. This mentality will *ruin* your experience as a collegiate golfer.

Personally, I see adversity as a combination of short, and long term challenges. Examples of short term challenges include facing a difficult situation on the golf course or a surprise assignment from your professor. Long term challenges include mastering fundamentals in all areas of your golf game, managing your academic and athletic calendar and building strength and conditioning in the gym.

Short term challenges are usually easy to handle. You simply identify the challenge, figure out a solution and implement your strategy. For example, we've all hit a tee shot into the trees, chipped out sideways and saved bogey. Simple. However, this simple short term adversity turns into something different if you risk hitting your next shot through the trees and compounding the problem. But that's a story for another time.

Long term challenges are tougher to manage because improvement comes much slower. For example, maybe you're trying to build physical strength to help increase club-head speed for more distance off the tee. If you've been in a workout program before you understand strength gains in the gym don't occur overnight. It takes time and consistent effort to realize significant improvements. Same with your golf skills. Creating world class short game skills requires incredible time and effort, and you may not even realize you're getting better during the process. Perseverance is about committing to the process, taking purposeful action day after day, month after month, year after year until one day you realize you've separated from your peers. Now you're competing with the select few willing to sacrifice what you've sacrificed. The select few disciplined enough to embrace a lifelong process. The select few who *persevered.*

So here's my suggestion, become a fighter in everything you do. And no, I'm not talking about MMA or boxing, I'm talking about everyday challenges. Work as hard as you can at practice, study for exams and prioritize homework. Run an extra mile, read another book, practice another hour. Become physically and mentally *STRONG*. Become the person seeking out challenges, struggle and discomfort. If you have a bad moment, bad day, bad week, don't worry about it. Come back stronger, keep scratching, keep clawing, keep *fighting*. If you become this person you won't wither in the face of adversity. You will smile knowing your entire life is about facing adversity, and *overcoming* it.

-Chapter Summary-

1. Recognize that everyone experiences hardships; it's your response to these challenges that matters most.

2. College golfers have demanding schedules both on and off the course; you must face this challenge head on. Developing a system to manage all aspects of your life on campus shapes who you'll become as a college golfer, and person in this world.

3. Handling adversity is a three-part process: accept the situation for what it is, then focus all your energy on what you can control, and finally, lead yourself to a favorable outcome.

4. Never seek the path of least resistance; this is a very dangerous habit.

5. Becoming resilient is a simple three-part process: lean into challenging situations, execute your process with 100% conviction, learn from the outcome and adjust accordingly. Repeat this process over and over and you'll become incredibly resilient.

7 CONFIDENCE, SELF-TALK & COURAGE

If I asked you to describe the most successful people you know regardless of age or profession, I imagine the word confidence would appear somewhere in the description. As athletes, we're constantly searching for and trying to maintain confidence as if it were the rarest commodity. Golfers it seems, are the quickest of all athletes to admit they've lost confidence or are "trying to find their confidence". Why is that? What is it about golf that requires so much confidence, and why are we so ready to admit when we've lost it?

The conversation about self-confidence must begin with a concept deeply rooted in the foundation of how we perceive ourselves, and that's *self-image.* Self-image is a tricky concept because our confidence varies from one situation to the next. We, as humans, are complicated and profoundly emotional beings. Our self-perceptions are fluid, influenced by the various environments we encounter and how we've managed these situations in the past. For example, maybe you're ultra confident on the golf course, but you're very uncomfortable speaking in front of crowds or exercising in front of others. If you're already ultra confident on the course, congrats, you're ahead of the curve. The truth is, most amateur golfers I work with freely admit they're lacking confidence in some area of their game.

Fortunately, there's a fix. This first section on self-confidence is all about reframing the way you see yourself on the course, and in the world. It starts with an understanding that you are **allowed** to create a self-image however you see fit. And this goes for all areas of life, not just golf. So what does that look like? If I asked you to describe yourself as a golfer what would you say? When I ask young players this question I often get responses like, "I'm ok off the tee but my short game really stinks.", or "I usually shoot somewhere in the 70's but I could easily shoot 82." The more confident amateurs I work with might say something like, "I feel pretty good about my game; everything's going well but there's certainly room for improvement." Any of these sound familiar?

Let me suggest an alternative method for thinking about yourself as a golfer. It starts by creating a vision of who you want to become, and then embodying the traits of what that person would say and do. For example, do you want to become an elite golfer? Do you want to be fit and healthy? Do you want to be a confident public speaker? If so, the first step is believing you're **already** that person, and then taking action accordingly.

Let's focus on the elite golfer. In any given situation, what would an elite golfer do? For example, what would an elite golfer do at practice? How would an elite golfer approach exercise and nutrition? What would an elite golfer do with extra time during the evening hours? Once you've decided that you're an elite golfer (regardless of your current skill level), these are the questions you must ask yourself every day, then act accordingly.

Would an elite golfer create a comprehensive practice plan attacking his weaknesses? Yes. Would an elite golfer approach fitness and nutrition like a professional athlete? Yes. Would an elite golfer study course management techniques and read about the mental game during his off hours at night? Yes. If you're unsure about how to implement the actions I'm describing, then it's your responsibility to learn. Being "elite" at anything requires tremendous discipline and resiliency. Therefore, you must embrace the personality and actions of an elite golfer long before you actually become one. *It's the quickest path to mastery.* So when someone asks you about your game, simply respond, "it feels great, I think I can win every time I tee it up."

You may be thinking "this is a great theory, but I struggle with confidence and it seems silly to say or think I'm elite." I certainly understand this perspective and have experienced it myself. Fortunately, there are actions and techniques you can implement to supercharge your self-image and solidify the belief that you're actually the person you've created in your mind.

The first strategy, embrace the work. There's simply nothing better for your self-image than tireless preparation. For example, if you lack confidence in your short-game but accept the challenge and go "all-in" on improving it, the sheer amount of attention you give your short-game will lead to improvement. As your skills improve, your confidence improves. *It can be that simple.* Take another example outside of golf, let's say you want to improve your body composition. Well, if you commit to lifting weights and cardiovascular training multiple times per week, what do you think will happen? Your body will start to change, and you'll feel better about the way you look. You may have to dial in your nutrition if you want those six-pack abs, but that's a conversation for another day. The point is, committing to the work and **actually doing it** is the first step toward building confidence in any given area. Are you ready to go all-in?

The next tool in your arsenal is a potent technique known as "anchoring". Anchoring is the process of capturing positive moments in your life and storing them securely in your subconscious. To put this into context, let's consider how I implement this strategy in my post-round routine. At the first opportunity (post-round), I find a quiet spot, settle in, and actively recall all the positive moments from my round. I focus solely on the best moments, tapping into the emotions I experienced on the course, and what I'm feeling in the present as I recall each moment. This isn't just reminiscing, it's a powerful strategy because your brain notices when you attach emotions to actions. When you attach a strong emotion to an action it instructs your brain to store that moment for future reference. The more positive moments you anchor, the greater your emotional reservoir to draw from when you need it most. But remember, this tool cuts both ways. If you anchor moments with negative emotion attached to them, your brain will dutifully store these as well. Continually anchoring negative actions and outcomes forces your brain to recall these moments when facing similar situations in the future. That said, anchoring positivity is a mighty tool, and with time, can reshape your worldview for the better.

Once I've firmly anchored all the positive moments from my round, I give myself a breather - maybe an hour or so. After this pause, I intentionally place my attention on those aspects of my game that didn't go as planned. I extract what lessons can be learned, make a point to work on those areas in my next practice session, then immediately discard them forever. I do this as unemotionally as possible, never judging or shaming myself in the process. The great players I work with almost never dwell on negative experiences; they simply use them for improvement and move on.

The next piece of this puzzle is avoiding negative conversation about your game. We've all been there, you're eating lunch with your playing partners discussing the round, and undoubtedly, someone is talking about how many three-putts they had, or how many balls they sent OB on a particular hole. Have you ever contributed to one of these conversations? I'm sure I know the answer. *You must develop the skill of avoiding these conversations.* If you're sitting with a group that's recalling all the bad shots of their round, simply acknowledge or laugh with them (or leave), but do not engage in recalling your bad moments. Think about it this way, when you participate in this type of recollection, you're not just rehashing your own mishaps, you're contributing to the negative "current" of the conversation. This amplifies negative anchoring, further embedding those unwanted memories deep into your subconscious while sabotaging your self-image. Do yourself a favor and avoid these conversations altogether.

Developing an elite self-image doesn't happen by chance, it's a skill to be cultivated like any other. Consider painting a vivid image of who you'll become across all areas of life, then commit to the actions that align with your new self-image. Practice the skill of anchoring positivity, and quickly move past moments that don't go your way. We'll cover self-confidence as it relates to on-course scenarios in the upcoming sections, but the foundation of genuine self-belief is rooted in the creation and commitment to your ultimate self-image. Remember, this is a process so consider aiming for 1% improvements day after day, week after week. If you stay accountable to the person you've chosen to become, that person will eventually be looking back at you in the mirror.

* * *

It's fair to say that everyone is humbled by this game at some point, professionals included. You may think all professional golfers are supremely confident, especially when you're watching the final round of a PGA or European Tour event on a Sunday afternoon. But that's misleading. If you're watching the final round you're only seeing the leaders who are probably having the best week of their year, or maybe even their life. What you don't see are the players who fell out of contention or shot 82 during their final round. Trust me, not everyone playing on Sunday is having a great round.

I have seen and heard many tour players speak negatively about their game following a poor round. The comments usually sound something like, "I don't know what happened, I just didn't have any confidence off the tee", or "my game felt good, but I had zero confidence on the greens today". So what could go so terribly wrong that a professional golfer loses confidence? The answer is simpler than you think. As golfers we recognize the importance of the many skills required to play great golf, and how quickly we can lose confidence in any one of them. However, regardless of the skill (tee ball, short game, putting, etc), the cause of the lost confidence is usually the same.

Let's examine the tee shot. When golfers lose confidence off the tee (regardless of their ability), there's a predictable sequence of events taking place. The first event, of course, is the bad tee shot. Now, depending on the severity of the miss the player could shrug it off, continuing the round unaffected. However, if the miss is significantly bad or the player isn't supremely confident, he may start to question his technique. The player may think "what horrific swing flaw just caused my ball to fly 30 yards out of bounds?". It doesn't matter the player may have already hit the previous four fairways, feeling confident about their swing. One poor swing can have a cascading (negative) effect on the next. We've all been there. You stand on the next tee thinking about what caused your previous miss. You think back to your range sessions, the previous holes, maybe a good swing thought you had earlier in the day, anything to get you back on track. But here's the truth, if you are thinking about how to "get back on track", you're already lost. You may think this is a positive mindset, but it's really just fear. Fear that you've lost your swing, fear that you've lost your confidence, fear that you've lost your ability to perform. Inevitably, the next tee shot flies offline and you're well on your way to "losing your confidence".

So what's the solution? Well, if you're like me you've experienced this "loss of confidence" during a round and the moment you putt-out on 18, you proceed directly to the driving range to "fix" the problem. You arrive at the range, put your bag down, pull out the driver, tee it high and rip it directly down your target line. The most beautiful tee ball imaginable. Followed directly by "why couldn't I do that on the course?". I am here to tell you, *you could have.*

Let's go back several steps in the process to the initial wayward shot. It doesn't matter how far offline or how embarrassing the result, your response must be the same regardless. *Acceptance.* That's right, assuming you did everything in your power to execute a perfect pre-shot routine and fully commit to the swing, you must accept the result understanding you're human and poor swings *do* occasionally happen, even to great players. Accepting the result means just that, you've accepted it and moved on. One component of confidence is trusting your ability to execute the next swing well, even after a bad result.

Let me ask you this, what's your mentality on the range after you hit several perfect tee shots in a row, then (randomly) hit one offline? Do you lose confidence? Do you question your mechanics? Do you panic? No, you simply tee it up again, refocus on the task and rip it down range. This is precisely the attitude necessary to alleviate doubt on the course. When you're hitting the (next) tee shot following a miss, you simply execute a perfect pre-shot routine, commit to the swing and let it go as if you were on the range. *Trust this process.* Thinking about mechanics, an old swing thought, or anything else, distracts you from the task at hand.

Golf is unique to other sports in that long time intervals occur between each shot. To me, this is what makes golf so difficult. Most other sports are reactionary in nature, meaning there's no time to think about a poor result. In fact, you may have to play both offense *and* defense. In these sports there isn't time to examine every detail of your previous efforts, you simply react to the environment and perform to the best of your ability. Your preparation leading up to the event is the greatest determinant of success. To that point, I try to make golf as reactionary as possible.

To make golf reactionary you must accept three undeniable truths. First, you're going to hit bad golf shots. Don't fight me on this, it's going to happen. Second, when you hit a poor shot you must accept the result and move on immediately without doubting yourself in the process. Third, you must have an elite pre-shot routine. If you struggle with any of these ideas you're falling behind. To make golf reactionary you must be focused on the task at hand, always. Lingering thoughts of previous failures infect your ability to think clearly on the present task, which is always the (current) target. Finally, you must have an elite pre-shot routine. When I say elite, I'm not talking about a pre-shot routine modeled after some tour player. I am saying you must have the ability to perform *your* pre-shot routine with clarity and decisiveness on every shot, without exception. Therefore, when you're engaged in your pre-shot routine you're reacting to the golf shot in it's entirety. Meaning, you select your target, choose the best shot for the situation, align your body, position the ball and perform the swing automatically. The best players in the world execute this process with extreme proficiency.

So what does this have to do with confidence? Well, confidence is defined as something you can count on, or believe in. So the more quality shots you hit, the more you believe in your swing. We know hitting quality shots requires a clear mind that's laser focused on the present task. You simply cannot focus your attention on the present task if you're thinking about a previous result. So clear your mind, execute the perfect pre-shot routine, commit to the shot and let it go. If you've done the work in preparation, you'll have the confidence to consistently execute great golf shots, round after round.

* * *

Maybe you're saying, "sure that sounds great coach, but what if I don't *believe* I can hit the next tee shot down the fairway?" Great question, and it leads directly to the second aspect of confidence, *self-talk*.

One of the great advantages of being human is the ability to create, manipulate and manifest original thoughts into reality. To my knowledge, we're the only creatures on earth with this ability. Your existence as a person is a combination of conscious and subconscious thoughts that manifest into actions that other people perceive, and vice versa. So what does this have to do with golf shots? Well, if you're not aware of what that voice in your head is saying, you should be. That voice is infinitely powerful, commanding your every action. It may be the single most important factor for your success as a golfer and person in this world. So again, what does it have to do with golf shots? *Everything*.

How do you speak to yourself on the golf course? Are you encouraging, confident, reassuring and forgiving? Or is your self-talk the more destructive type? Do you cuss yourself out, call yourself names, belittle and shame yourself, doubt yourself?

On one occasion I was implementing putting drills with my team and I noticed a player who was clearly struggling. He was working on 3-foot putts positioned in a circular fashion around the hole. As I watched from a distance, he missed one putt after another, becoming more and more frustrated after each miss. Mind you, he wasn't reading the putt or taking his time, he simply looked at the hole and made his stroke. Finally, after three or four consecutive misses and a flurry of words I choose not to repeat, I decided to intervene. I approached the player and asked how he was doing. "terrible!", he replied. So I asked why, full well knowing the answer. He said, "Coach, I can't make a putt and my stroke feels horrendous. I have no idea what's going on and I can't get the ball started on the correct line." Keep in mind, this player had a perfectly acceptable putting stroke and to my knowledge, hadn't struggled getting the ball on-line before that moment. So I removed a quarter from my pocket, threw it on the ground and positioned a ball 12 inches from the coin. Then, I instructed him to putt the ball over the coin without lining it up in any way. To his amazement, he hit the coin repeatedly (at least 10 in row). Ok I said, it's clear you can get your ball rolling online,

Right? He couldn't believe it. In less than one minute he was hitting every putt online without using the line on his ball or reading the putt. A miracle!

Next, we moved on to the 3-foot putting drill he was working on. I asked him to relax, be patient and read the putt as if he were on the course, giving himself every chance to make it. So he went through the process, holing the first putt, then the next five, and I eventually lost track after about 15 in a row. As each ball rolled over the edge, his hands loosened on the grip, his stroke becoming more fluid, his confidence returning. "How do you feel now?" I asked. "GREAT!" he said. Less than ten minutes before he was angry, negative and visually beaten. Now, he was excited, motivated, confident.

How is this transformation possible? I'm here to tell you it's 100% in your control. Let's back up to my player's first comment. I initially asked how he was doing. "Terrible!" he replied. So in that moment, his entire perspective on life was terrible. It didn't matter that it was a beautiful fall day in New Mexico, the golf course was absolutely perfect and he was living the dream of a college golfer in America. None of that mattered, he was "terrible" because he couldn't sink a three footer. I know, it seems ridiculous but this is the power your conscious mind has over your perspective. Regardless of your physical surroundings, your self talk determines your perspective on the outside world.

His next comment, "I can't get the ball started on the correct line" obviously wasn't true. All I had to do was interrupt his negative thought pattern, introduce a new target with a specific goal (roll it over the quarter), and voila, he's cured! So what happened to allow this transformation? I introduced a task that was easy enough for him to believe he could accomplish it. All of a sudden he was rolling the ball exactly where he wanted to, every time. He couldn't say "I can't start the ball online" because he was obviously doing it. Internally, he (probably) transitioned from "I can't get it started online" to "Ok, maybe I can get it started online" which initiated more positive self-talk and belief.

In the moment before I arrived, he was caught in a negative loop, each missed putt reinforced his belief that he couldn't start the putt online and his life was "terrible" because of it. When I asked how he was doing, the first word out of his mouth was "terrible" so he was clearly thinking this (or something worse) internally. However, with a basic putting drill and some positive reinforcement (from me) his overall mood transitioned from "terrible" to "great" in less than 10 minutes. The small accomplishment of rolling his ball over the quarter was all he needed to regain confidence. His stroke became more fluid and athletic and he attacked the drill with new found confidence. This was a complete turn around both mentally and physically. Ok, so how do you accomplish this turn around when you're on the course and not able to implement a drill? It starts by understanding how self-talk effects your current and future actions, then gaining control of how you speak to yourself in all situations.

Perhaps you've heard the term "manifest destiny". This refers to a person's ability to create an idea, cultivate it, believe in it, and eventually the idea becomes reality. The author, Napoleon Hill, had a different term for this called "autosuggestion"whereby the person (consciously) feeds his subconscious mind ideas and instructions for how he wants to live, and the subconscious mind directs his actions to create this (new) reality. There are also various types of meditation and hypnosis that serve similar purposes. Regardless of the method, these mental practices share a common strategy; consciously implement (positive) beliefs via self-talk to manifest desired outcomes.

Think about it like this, your conscious thoughts are instructions for your subconscious mind. If the general tone of your conscious self-talk is negative, your overall disposition on the golf course (and in life) may be very well be negative. Conversely, if your self-talk is generally positive, your approach to life is probably positive. Simple enough. To fully understand self-talk and apply it to golf, we need to examine short and long term situations.

First, let's examine self-talk in the short term. Picture yourself facing a difficult situation on the golf course. Maybe you're facing a situation that requires a high draw around trees to a tucked pin, and you don't love the high draw. Or, Maybe there's a hazard guarding the left side of the fairway and you've been pulling your tee shots all day (or pushing for you lefties). How will you handle this in real time? Will you approach these situations with a positive attitude? Or, is your self-talk something like this? "I've never hit the high draw well, this isn't going to end well." Or, "oh great, another water hazard down the left. We know where this ball is going." You may be laughing, but unfortunately I've heard (great) college players say similar comments *out loud*, so you know they're thinking about it internally. Predictably, the outcome is exactly how the player imagined it... bad. But what if you actually struggle with the high draw or you've been pulling your tee shots left? It doesn't matter, you must approach each situation with belief.

For example, you're facing the high draw but it's not your best shot. Your approach could be, "nice, another opportunity to improve on the high draw!" Or perhaps you say "this is a great opportunity to implement my work on the high draw. I've been waiting for this shot all day!"Obviously the positive self-talk is the better option, but why?

We know our subconscious mind controls certain actions like breathing and digestion. But certain physical activities can also become subconsciously controlled after many repetitions. For example, you don't have to think about taking each step when you walk, or controlling the pedals when driving a car. The same goes for your golf swing. After millions of swings you no longer require conscious direction of the movement. When we're playing our best golf we consciously decide on a shot, modify our address position to perform the shot (ball position, alignment, etc), then let our subconscious mind execute the swing. The swing itself isn't controlled through conscious thought, just like walking.

So here's the point, when you introduce negative self-talk into your pre-shot routine you're instructing your subconscious mind to produce a negative outcome. Sounds ridiculous, right? Nope, it's true. Negative self-talk has real impact on your physiology. When you're thinking positively your swing is smooth, aggressive and confident. When you think negatively your swing becomes tight, guarded, scared. When you think negatively, and worse yet, believe your negative thoughts, your shot (typically) does exactly what you feared it would, reinforcing the belief that you cannot hit the shot in the first place. It's a self fulfilling prophecy. However, If you approach the situation positively, no matter what shot you're hitting, you're instructing your subconscious mind that you *can* hit this shot. So your swing stays fluid, aggressive and confident. This gives you the best chance at executing the shot and overcoming your fear of past failures. If the shot comes off poorly, *who cares*. You did everything in your power to execute the shot and you'll be better off for it down the road.

Maintaining positive self-talk on the golf course is imperative for your success. But you may be saying, "coach I struggle with negative self-talk, how do I change the narrative in my head? The answer, you change your entire approach to life.

Look, I'm certainly not here to tell you how to live your life, but I struggled with negative self-talk and eventually overcame it, so my experience could help you. During a particularly rough period of time in my 20's I wasn't playing good golf and seemingly everything in life was going the wrong direction. Every time I drove my car I experienced bad traffic, my (fitness) gym was always crowded and I couldn't exercise how I wanted, my friends were doing well and I just couldn't catch a break. I was mad at the world. Of course, none of these things were actually true, it was simply a matter of perspective. Over a period of time my general outlook on life had turned negative, and therefore, everything in my life was negative. I was looking for reasons to be upset. Our subconscious mind responds to our conscious instructions whether they're positive or negative. Therefore, your outlook on life is completely within your control, whether it's good or bad.

Thankfully I recognized this pattern and began searching for a cure. I read countless psychology books, consulted trusted friends and family and did everything in my power to inspire personal change. I became painfully aware of every thought, negative or positive. Over time, I trained myself to stop what I was doing when negative thoughts entered my mind. I would recognize the negative thought, then consciously redirect my mind to something positive. For example, if I was heading into rush hour traffic I would think about it first, visualizing what was ahead and accepting it for what it was. Then I searched for ways to improve my traffic experience. I began listening to audio books and podcasts, turning the experience into something positive. One scenario after another I changed my negative outlook to positive and my internal narrative started changing. After months of (self) therapy and conscious devotion to change, I became incredibly positive. I was actively helping others with similar issues and seeking out challenges wherever I could. I had changed my life.

So if you're struggling with negative self-talk on the course, you may want to examine your approach to life. For example, I had the pleasure of coaching a student athlete that almost never showed negative emotion on the course. Regardless of his position on the leaderboard, he always told me he was doing "great". He never told me about the previous hole's bad break or some terrible putting situation. He simply said, "I'm doing great, coach". It didn't matter if he was 6 under, or 6 over, he was always doing great. Not surprisingly, his approach to life (and his tireless work ethic) inspired great confidence in his game. He knew he had a great life, therefore he had nothing to lose on the course. If he didn't perform well, he simply worked harder, never losing sight of his goals. This attitude carried over to everything he did off the course as well. He was the same guy at 6 a.m. team workouts, 2 p.m team practice, 4 a.m. bus rides to tournaments, it didn't matter. He applied the same positive, accepting mindset to everything he did. He was in fact, great.

I know it's challenging, but you *can* make a change. When you encounter tough situations or aren't playing your best, don't let your mind wander to the negative. If you do have a negative thought that's ok, but do your best not to say it out loud, especially to your coach. Verbalizing a thought gives it life. If you're thinking negatively, stop yourself, recognize the negative thought then change the narrative to something positive. You must be disciplined with this process. Performing well under pressure requires clear, positive thoughts and a definite course of action. There is no place for negativity.

The same goes for all scenarios in life. If your initial reaction to a situation is negative, stop yourself right there. How can you turn this situation around? Remember, *you* are in charge of your thoughts, do not negotiate with your mind. You decide how you speak to yourself. So why not use this incredible power for good? You are allowed to be confident, strong and empowered. Instead of saying "oh great, I got screwed again," say something like "here we go, challenge accepted!". Do this every time you face adversity and you'll change your life. You will become mentally stronger than anyone you know. Then, as you engage and overcome challenges you'll become what every golfer desires. You will become *self-confident.*

* * *

In my experience, self-confidence on the golf course develops through tireless (physical) preparation and positive, unbreakable self-talk. However, I know some of you still aren't convinced and I hear you speaking through the page as I write this. You are saying, "coach, I still have doubts. I have doubts on the golf course, I have doubts when I speak publicly, I have doubts about exercise,

I have doubts about everything." Good, that means you're human. Fear and doubt are emotions we all feel, and you're stuck with them for the rest of your life. You see, many thousands of years ago humans needed fear to identify, evade and escape predation. Fear is hard wired into our DNA and it's not going anywhere. Unfortunately, fear and doubt have become something entirely different in the modern age. We no longer run from bears or sabertooth tigers. No it's much worse, now we conjure up fears through societal conditioning, and for some, these fears never go away.

So how do you develop fear in the first place? I imagine it starts with your parents who through no fault of their own, instilled in you some basic guidelines for life. Maybe you've heard your parents say "be careful out there," or "don't do anything I wouldn't do," or maybe even "play smart today, don't take unnecessary risks." These seemingly benign remarks lodge themselves into your subconscious and (can) dictate your actions without you knowing it. Therefore, when facing difficult situations your subconscious tells you to "be careful," or "don't do anything your parents wouldn't do," and maybe even "don't do that, it's way too risky." Sound familiar?

So, how do *you* handle challenging situations? Do you commit to a solution and move forward aggressively? Or, do you feel the fear, doubt your ability and simply "try not to screw up." If you you're nodding your head yes to the latter, don't be ashamed, you're certainly not alone. Fear of failure is the #1 reason golfers don't succeed. Perhaps you're afraid of the sand trap, the high draw, hitting in front of crowds, missing the short putt, or any number of situations you face on the course. When confronted with these challenges you tighten up and "try not to screw it up." As you know, this never ends well.

In my experience, self-doubt is usually a symptom of faulty preparation and (or) performance anxiety. For example, faulty preparation eventually leads to situations on the course you simply cannot handle. When you don't have the requisite skill to handle a difficult shot you get nervous and tighten up, typically leading to a bad result. But maybe you prepare very well and still feel anxious with particular shots. Perhaps you're afraid of what your peers will think if you miss a short putt. Or, maybe you skulled a bunker shot in front of your teammates last weekend, and now every time you're in the sand you feel anxious.

Getting past fear of failure is twofold. First, you identify your weakness (mental or physical) and commit to overcoming it. This element of the process is nonnegotiable. If you choose to ignore weaknesses in your game (or in your life), they will fester, becoming infinitely worse. Second, you embrace the final and most important element of self-confidence; *courage.*

Courage is the ability to attack difficult situations without hesitation. In other words, you must embrace challenging moments as opportunities to grow as a person. Break free of the conservative mold you're accustomed to. When faced with adversity or an important situation, trust your preparation and move forward aggressively. What do you have to lose? I know from experience, backing away from challenges or approaching them with the "trying not to screw it up" attitude leaves you empty inside. You will be thinking about these moments many hours after they occur wondering, "why didn't I just go for it?" You see, "going for it" is the remedy for fear and uncertainty.

Now, "going for it" doesn't mean approaching every situation recklessly, that's not what I'm saying at all. Rather, as you progress through your golf career the courses become more difficult and you'll face challenges on the most basic shots (tee shots, putting, bunkers, etc.). You have no choice but to embrace the challenge and give it everything you've got. It simply doesn't matter if you make a mistake, that's part of the process and your number one tool for improvement. I tell players all the time, don't measure success on the course by your score, measure it by your thought process throughout the round. Were you fully committed to each shot? Did you embrace challenges and proceed aggressively? Or, did you let nerves and fear get the best of you?

Mark my words, you will face challenging moments throughout your life, and those moments define you as a person. You either accept challenges and move forward or you don't. Either option instructs your subconscious how to direct your actions in the future.

Of the many challenges I've faced throughout my life, one stands alone as the most personally defining. As a 29 year old adult I returned to college and joined an NCAA golf program. I was older than everyone on the team, including the coach. Looking back, it was the best decision of my life but at the time it was a very difficult choice. I had already played professional golf tournaments, started a career (away from golf), lived among friends and family, and was having a productive life. However, I knew something was missing and I had to make a change. But returning to school at age 29? That decision comes with many questions. What would my peers think about me returning to school? How would this decision effect my financial situation? Would I have to cash in retirement savings to make the move, basically resetting my financial future back to square one? Would my new teammates accept an older person on the team? These uncertainties led to many sleepless nights in the weeks and months leading up to the initial semester back at school. All I knew was I wanted another chance at tournament golf and finishing my college degree was a top priority. So I took a leap of faith. I believed in my ability to mesh with teammates and set a great example. I knew pursuing my dream of playing professional golf and finishing my degree was the correct course of action. I simply needed the courage to do it. So I did. I humbled myself and committed everything I had to the golf program and academics. It was the best experience and decision of my life, and I wouldn't be speaking to you now without it.

So next time you're facing a challenge, take a leap of faith and believe in your ability. It doesn't matter if you fail, that's part of the process. What matters is you tried. Not only did you try, you gave 100% effort. When you see challenges as opportunity for growth, you have nothing to lose. Regardless of the outcome, you're gaining experience and becoming stronger and more confident in the process. If you become this person, you will build unbreakable self-confidence and belief. You will never shy away from challenges and you'll embrace opportunities as they emerge in your life. So be brave, be humble, and above all else, *be courageous.*

-Chapter Summary-

1. You are allowed to create whatever self-image you desire.

2. Create a vision for who you wish to become and embody the traits of that person.

3. Go all-in on improving your physical and mental skills.

4. Anchor positive moments from all areas of life.

5. Avoid negative conversation about your game.

6. Make golf reactionary by using a three-step process: manage expectations regarding outcomes, believe 100% in your pre-shot routine, and accept results immediately.

7. Use self-talk to your advantage. By encouraging and empowering yourself you can handle any challenging situation.

8. Have the courage to confront difficult situations. You will continue facing more and more challenging environments as you ascend in this game, your only choice is to believe in your ability and go for it.

8 PRACTICE

My theory on practice contains three fundamental attributes; work ethic, purpose and plan. If you master these attributes your game will accelerate faster than you ever thought possible. But practice isn't just showing up and going through the motions, it's a skill to be developed like all other skills.

My brother Paul would tell you I didn't always embrace practice. Unlike him I didn't have an obsessive, burning desire to master the fundamentals (of everything) as a kid. I just wanted to play. I have many memories of my brother practicing his golf swing in the front yard of our childhood home in Michigan. A good portion of those memories include a snow covered lawn and we wouldn't be seeing grass for several months, let alone playing golf. But that didn't matter to him, he saw an opportunity to improve and regardless of the conditions, he got after it. My brother has love for the game, and while he didn't become a professional golfer, he used his unrelenting work ethic to become a successful businessman in his adult life.

Not everyone is blessed with an unstoppable work ethic like my brother. A great work ethic is typically forged over time as you master the skills of discipline and sacrifice. In my view, your work ethic is a direct reflection of your ability to prioritize your time. So I'll ask you again, what are you willing to sacrifice to reach your full golf potential? Will there be moments when you're tired, bored, frustrated and distracted? Yes. Will there be other activities you'd rather be doing instead of grinding out bunker shots in the rain? Probably. But these moments define you as a golfer. These moments, if taken advantage of, give you an edge over your competition. And what's the consequence of not developing this type of work ethic? You simply won't stay competitive with other players your age who are already this committed.

In my experience there are three types of golfers on (high quality) college teams; good, great and elite. "Good" players typically have plenty of talent but don't work hard in practice and never reach their full potential. Their college career is underwhelming, rarely traveling with the top 5 and almost never challenge for individual tournament victories. "Great" players typically have upper level talent matched with a very good work ethic. They are very competitive, consistently finish in the top 20 and occasionally win the individual portion of tournaments. "Elite" players (typically) have world class talent paired with a very good to elite work ethic. These players consistently challenge for tournament victories, earn prestigious awards at the end of the year and (some) continue on to professional golf. Elite college players are easy to spot and they typically make the transition to professional golf with relative ease. For example, the Ben Hogan award is given each year to the most outstanding NCAA (Division 1) male collegiate golfer. Past winners of this award include John Rahm (twice), Rickie Fowler, Patrick Cantlay and Viktor Hovland, just to name a few. These players dominated the college game, making a seamless transition to the PGA Tour. What do these players have in common? Elite talent matched with an elite work ethic.

It should be noted that if you're not someone with "elite" talent, that's ok. I'm using a broad brush to categorize players here, and certainly there are golfers who don't have elite, or even great talent who work *tirelessly* and become very competitive college and professional golfers. However, this is rare and regardless of your talent level you must have an elite work ethic to ascend to the highest levels of this game. This is non-negotiable.

Once you've developed the work ethic you must learn how to practice with purpose to maximize your potential. My general philosophy on practice developed over many years working with great players and seeing firsthand which habits led to improvement and which did not. Most coaches I know tell their players to practice with purpose, and yes it's cliche, but it's the *truth*. Comprehensive proficiency in all areas of the game requires time, discipline and accountability each and every day. If you intend on being an elite college and professional golfer you simply cannot afford wasted practice time. So what does it mean to practice with purpose? Having purpose (for anything) means having a reason or direction for taking action. So what's your direction when you practice?

In my view, too many (competitive) amateur golfers spend the majority of their practice time "fixing" a swing flaw when that time could be used much more efficiently. In my experience, young players view practice as a time to fix a problem, instead of learning and executing new shots.

As you begin developing a practice strategy consider the following questions. How often do you check your fundamentals (alignment, ball position, posture, etc.)? How often do you hit shots to targets implementing your entire pre-shot routine? Do you work on learning new shots? If so how often? How about your short game, do you routinely seek out difficult lies and stances during your practice sessions, or do you stick to flat lies from the fairway cut? Do you hit pitch shots with multiple clubs to the same target (with success)? How's your spin control using various clubs from difficult lies around the green? How about bunker play? Do you execute the chunk and run, high spinner, and plugged shots with different clubs? Or, is your practice time devoted to (robotically) hitting balls in search of the the perfect swing? If you're the robot, you need to listen carefully.

I don't believe the swing requires technical or mechanical analysis every time you're on the range (quite the opposite). Think about it this way, if you and I were playing catch with a ball, would you be analyzing your arm motion each time you threw me the ball? Does a professional soccer player think about kicking mechanics as she attempts to score a goal? Or even simpler yet, as you walk down the street do you think about the intricacies of your gait cycle? Of course not. We let our subconscious mind and athletic talent handle these tasks. Can we agree that thinking mechanically about any of those activities (while attempting them) would lead to poor results? I think so. However, for some reason golfers are conditioned to believe there's something wrong with their swing if the shot result isn't perfect every time. But what happens if you trip while walking down the road? Do you question the way you walk? Do you hire a professional walking coach? Do you analyze every detail of your gait cycle? No, you don't. So don't think about practice as a time to perfect your swing. Rather, think about practice as a time to perfect *golf shots.*

Ok so how should you practice to perfect golf shots? First and foremost, creating and executing a practice plan is essential for your growth as a competitive golfer. Practice plans vary from player to player, but all great professional and collegiate players I've been around have pre-determined tasks for their daily work. For example, the first hour of practice could be dedicated to your full-swing. Set a timer and use that hour for whatever full-swing work you need. For me, a typical full-swing block was 15-20 minutes warming up and "feeling" a swing thought, then utilizing the remaining 40-45 minutes hitting shots to targets going through my entire pre-shot routine while changing the shot-shape and target periodically throughout. This fully engaged my mind and kept me focused on the task. Once the hour is up, I moved on to the next phase of practice, regardless of how good or bad the full-swing practice was. Simple.

Short game practice is no different. I typically do contact drills for 10-15 minutes with multiple clubs, ensuring a quality strike for each combination of club and ball position. The rest of my time is dedicated to creating shots from various lies and stances, rarely hitting the same shot more than 3 times. A great short game requires creativity so you must seek out difficult lies and situations in practice. There's simply no other way to develop the skills necessary for every scenario you'll face on the course.

How about wedge practice? Because distance control is paramount with wedges, you'll need to spend significant time hitting shots to short and intermediate targets. This is one of the only occasions I use "volume" practice, hitting hundreds of balls to various targets and not necessarily going through my pre-shot routine for every shot. In my experience, the best wedge players can control and manipulate trajectory and spin with multiple clubs for every distance within 150 yards. For example, can you hit a 100 yard shot with three different wedges, allowing you to attack targets with varying flight and spin for all situations (wind, pin placement, hazards, etc)? The best wedge players I've worked with can do this with relative ease. Mastering the wedge game requires time, and going through your entire pre-shot for every swing may not be the best strategy for success.

That said, to ensure proper alignment and ball position you should periodically integrate your pre-shot routine as you execute your wedge practice.

I've mentioned pre-shot routine several times already, so let's discuss it. I always include my pre-shot routine in each area of practice. If you're going to execute a pre-shot routine in tournaments, you better get used to doing it in practice. Your pre-shot routine significantly affects your ability to execute quality golf shots, especially under pressure. A great pre-shot routine calms and clears the mind, allowing full commitment to the task. On the other hand, a sloppy pre-shot routine leads to confusion, anxiety and poor shot making under pressure. Jack Nicklaus once said that he never hits a range ball without executing his pre-shot routine first. Jack understands the significance of a great pre-shot routine, not only calming the mind but ensuring all aspects of his setup occur automatically. Everyone's pre-shot is different, but if you study great players you'll notice one common trait among their routines; *decisiveness*. This entire section on practice is about purpose and discipline and a quality pre-shot routine requires both. The best golf shots occur when you direct your mind with precise, clear instructions for the task at hand. My pre-shot routine was simple and effective (for me) and goes like this; first, I select the appropriate target depending on the situation (pin location, hazards, wind, etc.). Next, I select the appropriate shot-shape and trajectory while standing behind the ball visualizing the shot until it's crystal clear in my mind. So clear that I can see the shot traced in color as I look out to the target. Once the shot-shape is clear in my mind I execute several practice swings feeling the exact motion and tempo required for the shot (draw, fade, high, low, etc.). When I'm totally confident in my feel, I address the ball and execute the shot. For years I have rehearsed my pre-shot routine for all types of shots so the aspects of setup (aim, ball position, posture, grip, etc.) occur naturally for each shot. But this efficiency doesn't happen overnight and a great pre-shot routine is a perishable skill. In other words, if you don't rehearse your pre-shot in practice it becomes less efficient in tournaments, leading to poor execution and wasted shots. Create a pre-shot routine specific to your physical rhythm (fast, methodical, etc.), rehearse it until it's automatic and utilize it every time you practice.

At this point you might be wondering about drills. My opinion on drills is simple, if you need work with a specific shot or skill go ahead and implement the appropriate drill. Repetition *is* part of the learning process and an important tool for golfers. A word of caution, hitting the same shot repeatedly for long periods of time (eventually) loses value. I recommend hitting 3-4 shots while working on the skill, then hit the next 3-4 shots implementing your full pre-shot routine. Take time between shots to get out of mechanical mode, and back into creative mode. This goes for putting, short game and full-swing drills. Also, don't get stuck working with the same drills over and over. Research new drills online, work with teammates and coaches and always look for new ways to improve your skills.

Now that we've covered my general philosophy on practice lets move on to the plan itself. First, when creating a practice plan start by writing down all the requisite skills necessary to play elite level golf (refer to the beginning of the chapter for ideas). Don't worry about creating a perfect list, just start with the basics (full swing, short game, putting, etc), then add more specific skills as you go along. As you create daily or weekly plans scan your skills list for potential weaknesses in your game, highlighting those areas first in your daily plan. Remember, you must be brutally honest with your self-evaluation. Need extra work from the sand? Struggle with a knockdown 5-iron? Despise downhill lies? Regardless of the area(s) of need, dedicate a section of time for that skill in your daily plan.

We are all unique individuals so there's no perfect plan for everyone. Some people may like complex, highly detailed routines planned down to the minute. Others may thrive with a more generalized approach allowing more flexibility during their practice session. Just remember, having a plan is better than not having a plan, and as usual, this is a skill that must be developed and mastered over time.

Self-evaluation should be the starting point of a quality practice plan, and for that reason you should be using a statistical program to track and analyze each area of your game. If you're not tracking your stats and using that data to direct your practice, you're falling behind. There are several good (free) programs available online as well as paid subscriptions to more advanced applications. Some paid programs allow you to compare your stats with other college and professional golfers, offering invaluable data on your strengths and weaknesses. I don't believe you can be an elite level player in today's era without analyzing your stats and using them to direct your practice. Yes, it's extra work and may seem distracting at first, but tracking your stats allows you to understand your game at a much deeper level.

So what if you don't use a practice plan? Well, simply practicing hard and working on the fundamentals *will* lead to improvements in your game. However, for most players this method loses value over time. One possible consequence of not using a plan is falling into the same practice pattern you always use. Perhaps you know what I'm talking about? You arrive at the course, hit a bucket, go through your favorite putting drill, maybe hit a few (easy) pitch shots, and you're off. I have seen this a million times, even with high quality amateurs. This routine may lead to short term improvement, but eventually you'll fall behind your competitor who's implementing a comprehensive plan addressing all areas of the game. As you progress as a competitive golfer, the courses become more and more difficult and the demands on your game increase exponentially. You will face varying landscapes, grasses and course layouts all designed to challenge your abilities. If your game is one-dimensional, meaning you're only good at the limited skills you practice, you simply won't have the necessary shots to handle the most difficult courses.

Finally, how do discipline and accountability fit into this conversation about practice? Well, it's everything. You are accountable for your game, no one else. Evaluating your game, then creating and implementing strategies to overcome weaknesses requires discipline. Staying after practice for extra work while your friends and teammates retire for the evening requires discipline. Sacrificing the necessary time and energy to develop elite level skills, requires incredible discipline. If you truly want to maximize your talent and become an elite golfer, you must hold yourself accountable for each and every practice session. Make no mistake, someone is out there sacrificing everything. Someone is doing the work. Are you that someone?

* * *

I admit, there *is* a time and place for technical swing analysis. For example, if you're still mastering certain fundamentals of the swing and short game you should spend time working with your coach or professional. You should also learn how the club-face/swing-path relationship affects your ball flight because this will help you identify issues when you're working alone on the range. And yes, even the best players occasionally need technical/mechanical help with a swing flaw. However, I recommend getting out of this "fixing" phase as soon as possible and there's a specific reason why. Now, you'll have to bear with me as I discuss some basic physiology, but I believe it's important for you to understand how we learn physical skills and what it means for your performance.

According to a study by Fitts and Posner (1967), humans use a three stage process when learning physical tasks and it's important to progress through the stages to ensure peak performance. Let's briefly examine the three stages so you have an understanding of where you are in the process, and how to progress accordingly.

Stage one, cognitive. During the cognitive stage you're typically working with a coach or professional learning the fundamentals of a movement while discussing technique and theory. During this phase you use teaching aids, mirrors, video, and plenty of verbal feedback from the coach. You are simply acquiring information about the skill while simultaneously creating a new movement pattern of your own.

Stage two, associative. The associative stage can be viewed as the awkward stage, and is typically the most challenging. For golfers, this stage can be painfully slow because you are consciously integrating the new information into your old swing pattern. This process requires extreme focus and thousands of (correct) repetitions to achieve the desired change.

Stage three, autonomous. This is the stage we're all striving for, where movement becomes automatic. There is far less cognitive energy used in this stage, largely because the movement itself is highly trained and reliable. You are not thinking about the movement in segments, simply reacting subconsciously to your intended outcome. In this case, the desired shot.

I believe most, if not all, sports psychologists would agree that autonomous mode is one factor (of several) allowing athletes to enter a "flow state". In other words, a state of mind where the athlete performs at his/her best while not consciously aware of the specific physical movements required by their sport. They are simply seeing and reacting to their current environment.

So why is this important, and what is it doing in a section about practice? Two reasons; first, when you decide to embark on a physical swing change, regardless of the magnitude of the change, you are entering into the associative stage of learning. Anytime you are consciously thinking about a segment of your swing while trying to execute the shot, you're in associative mode. Transitioning from associative learning into autonomous action can take many weeks or months. So you need to consider the consequences of this type of practice before you embark on it. Why? Because the very nature of associative learning could require tremendous amounts of time, and you may need to sacrifice other areas of your practice to achieve the desired swing change. Ok, that's fair enough right? Well, you also need to consider where you are in your competitive season. For obvious reasons you wouldn't want to commit to a swing change with important events on the near horizon. Occasionally, golfers have to patch together their game until the end of the competitive season, then implement the swing change during their non-competitive season.

The second reason this learning model is important is to understand which mode of learning you're in, then practice accordingly. For example, if you are in the cognitive or associative mode of learning, you should be spending the majority of your time and effort on the specific movement pattern you're trying to perfect. If there's time, work on other areas of your game, but if you're in the off-season you can spare a few short game sessions to perfect the new skill. However, if your swing patterns are fundamentally sound and you're operating in autonomous mode, you need to be careful about how you practice. Autonomous mode requires far less cognitive effort, and if you're not practicing with a purpose (hitting to targets, creating shots, etc.), you can create problems that aren't actually there. I know this may sound crazy but here's a scenario I've come across many times working with college golfers.

There are several team members on the range hitting balls. Maybe there's a conversation going on between shots or perhaps they're listening to music while they work through the bag. Inevitably, one of the players loses focus and begins hitting wayward shots. As I watch, the player becomes more and more frustrated as the shots get worse over time. At some point in this process the player gets overwhelmed with frustration and finally calls for my assistance. Typically I hear something like, "coach, can you check my swing I have no idea what's going on here". I can't tell you how many times I've been through this (but it's a lot), and the fix is almost always the same. First, I ask the player his purpose for the shot he's practicing, and not surprisingly, most of the time the player admits he's lost track of his purpose and needs to focus. Next, I ask the player to walk me through the shot he's about to hit, describing in detail the set-up, trajectory, curve, and associated target. Lastly, I ask the player to hit the shot executing a full pre-shot routine as if they were on the golf course. Amazingly, after refocusing on the task the player regains full control of his swing and ball strike. No mechanical change or technical analysis, simply refocusing on the task.

Ok, so what happens to the player who loses focus but there isn't a coach there to help them get back on track? Well, there's an alternate reality to this scenario where the player continues hitting poor shots one after another until he can no longer handle the frustration and quits for the day. Perhaps the player goes home thinking he has a serious mechanical problem with his swing. Maybe the player schedules a lesson with his swing coach or sends a video to a friend for analysis. The coach or friend gives feedback about the player's swing (whether it's warranted or not) and now the player is regressing back into associative mode to work on a swing flaw. When in reality, there was nothing wrong with the player's swing, they simply lost focus due to poor practice habits.

Look, golf is hard enough on its own but it gets infinitely more difficult when you lose focus, and worse yet, confidence. This is why you must practice with focus and purpose. The focused, creative mindset is ideal for practice because it simulates your mindset on the golf course while keeping your swing in autonomous mode.

My intent with this section isn't breaking down your next practice session in detail. Rather, I want you to adopt a practice philosophy where attacking weaknesses is the #1 priority, followed closely by learning and executing new shots and mastering your pre-shot routine. Remember, competing at the highest level requires proficiency off the tee, accuracy with iron shots from varying conditions (including precise distance control), ability to create and execute short game shots from difficult lies using multiple clubs, and of course putting with excellent distance control and confidence. Oh and let's not forget maintaining a positive, controlled mindset. How are you going to master all of these skills if the majority of your practice time is spent "fixing" a swing flaw? Hope you have spare time!

* * *

If you're ready to dive into practice but need some help, I recommend reading "The Practice Manual" by Adam Young. Within this resource you'll find information on technical analysis, ball flight laws, strategies to improve distance control and shot creation, all while organizing your practice sessions like a pro.

I also recommend reading "The Short Game Bible" by Dave Pelz (Phil Mickelson's former short game coach). Pelz explains exactly which short game shots to hit in every situation (and why), while offering detailed advice on shot technique. This is a great resource for not only learning short game techniques, but guiding your short game practice sessions as well.

-Chapter Summary-

1. Build a practice philosophy with the following attributes:work ethic, purpose and plan.

2. Regardless of your talent level, you must develop an elite work ethic to ascend to the highest levels of this game.

3. Comprehensive proficiency in all areas of the game requires time, discipline and accountability each and every day.

4. Use the majority of your practice time to learn and develop new shots as opposed to fixing a flaw.

5. Creating and executing a practice plan is essential for your growth as a competitive golfer.

9 COMPETITION

My experience with tournament competition dates back to the early 1990's when I only carried 6 clubs and used an old fashioned pull-cart to carry my bag. My first pair of golf shoes were actually baseball cleats and I definitely had an extendable ball retriever. I had no idea how to manage a golf course properly or read a green, I simply wanted to play and compete. From that humble start I was fortunate to compete in hundreds of golf tournaments including junior golf, high school, college and pro, playing with just about every type of golfer imaginable. I've witnessed many different ways to succeed in competition and developed a system of my own along the way. Of course, every golfer is unique in personality and skill, but the best players I've been around share similar mental and physical characteristics allowing for consistently good tournament results. In my view, competing at your best is a three-part process including the following variables; preparation, tournament mindset, and managing expectations and distractions. Keep in mind your strategy can differ from mine or your teammate's and that's ok, simply consider the following information and apply it to your game as you see fit.

Preparation

It is apparent to me that preparation is the #1 predictor of tournament performance for most competitive golfers. If that weren't true, the most talented player in the field would win every event. But we know that's not how golf works. Golf rewards players who master the physical skills, manage the course with clear and precise decision making, and execute shots with unbreakable self-confidence and courage. Remember, great decision making, self-confidence and courage have little to do with talent, and you can build physical skills with a great practice plan and relentless work ethic.

To that point, I have to mention the importance of discipline and accountability in regards to preparation. The fact is, discipline and accountability are the foundation of preparation and without them, you simply won't unlock your full potential as a golfer. I want you to think about your practice routine and answer the following questions; how much *actual* time do you spend working on your weaknesses and mastering golf shots? Conversely, how much time do you spend chatting with teammates, looking at your phone or hitting shots without purpose? How about your time away from the course? Are you studying how great players approach the game? Do you analyze your stats and read books about course management and the mental game? If this sounds like a lot, it is. Just remember, only 3% of high school players make NCAA division 1 golf teams, and less than 1% of all college players become professional golfers.

My suggestion, approach this task one day at a time. Each morning renew your commitment to discipline and accountability and prioritize the actions you believe necessary for success. Think of each day as an opportunity to squeeze every ounce out of your talent and ability. Prepare for the upcoming event as if it were the most important event of your life, *because it is.* If you want to join the tiny percentage of elite golfers in the world you need to prepare accordingly, and that process starts *today.*

One particular golfer I coached many years ago comes to mind when discussing preparation. He worked hard on and off the course and tournament performance was very important to him. He was a true range rat, hitting bucket after bucket in search of the perfect swing. You would occasionally find him on the short-game area or executing a putting drill, but his main focus was hitting balls. However, his range sessions weren't necessarily devoted to mastering the pre-shot routine or executing golf shots, instead, he always seemed to be working on a swing flaw or implementing a new technique he heard or read about the day before.

As a young coach I didn't have the conviction I have now, and I often found myself enabling this process when I should have redirected his focus to pre-shot routine and executing purposeful golf shots. Not surprisingly, these poor practice habits eventually caught up with this player at a tournament during our fall season. The team was on the course for the opening round and I met up with him on his 4th hole. It was a difficult par four requiring a precise tee shot with his driver and he was considering his options. He seemed very indecisive about the shot and I could tell his confidence was waning. Finally, after about 3-4 minutes of consideration he decided on a shot and began his routine. I'll never forget what happened next. As he addressed the ball, he was noticeably uncomfortable. He was fidgeting with the grip, shuffling his feet and looking out to the fairway over and over again until finally, he stopped moving altogether, seemingly frozen in time staring down at the ball. I don't know how long he stared at that ball but it felt like an eternity. *Finally*, after an uncomfortable amount of time he woke up from his trance, looked at me and said "Coach, I don't know what the hell I'm doing here." I couldn't help but burst out laughing and seeing my reaction, he started laughing as well. It was obvious he had no idea what he was doing with the shot, his swing, his setup or anything else for that matter. All those hours on the range searching for the perfect swing achieved one thing, he was very good at *searching* for the perfect swing, not executing golf shots.

This is precisely why practicing with purpose is so important for your development as a competitive golfer. After all, the most important aspect of tournament golf *is executing golf shots*. Not your teammates, your gear, your coach or anything else that doesn't directly impact your ability to execute a great shot. The key to executing golf shots in competition is clear and precise decision making, and a decisive pre-shot routine inspiring confidence and belief in the shot. These skills develop over time as you implement your tournament routine in every aspect of practice including the range, short-game area, putting green and practice rounds between events.

I will say it's very difficult to make clear, precise decisions while executing a perfect pre-shot routine if you don't believe in your ability to hit the shot in the first place. With that in mind, consider the following questions as you get ready for your next event. Do you have a quality, repeatable "stock" shot you implement for most tee-shots and fairway iron shots? Are you proficient from common short game areas (all shots within 10 yards of the green including bunkers)? Do you have basic course management skills? Do you have a rock solid pre-shot routine for every shot? Do you putt with confidence and belief in your stroke? Do you understand expectations and control your emotions under pressure? These are the bedrock characteristics of the best players I've played against and coached, and in my opinion, maintaining these basic skills is the foundation of good tournament preparation.

Tournament Mindset

There are many ideas and books written about the optimal mindset for competition. Perhaps you've heard terms like "flow state" or "the zone", or competing in "the arena". Regardless of the name, most of these strategies involve similar tactics like calming and quieting the mind, staying present in the moment and being task oriented, all to execute physical actions without doubt or analytical thoughts about the action itself. To be fair, these are important concepts and you should explore each of them for yourself. However, before you can enter “the zone” you need an understanding of the foundational tournament mindset which includes the following two concepts; overcoming pressure and extreme ownership of your game.

Let's start with pressure because it's usually the first thing people speak about when discussing tournament golf. I'll begin by saying pressure is different for everyone because it's an intrinsic characteristic. In other words, we create and interpret pressure in our own way. For the competitive golfer, pressure comes from many directions. First, you have your own expectations for performance. After all, tournament performance is the key to advancing in this game, whether you're in high school, college or on tour. There's also pressure to perform well for your teammates and coach. For most, team golf is significantly different than the normal individual stroke play events you're accustomed to. In most cases you'll have to earn a position on the travel squad through team qualifying. I've heard college golfers say many times team qualifying is much more difficult than the tournament itself. In fact, many good players can't overcome the pressure of qualifying and never fulfill their potential as a competitive golfer. Then there's the tournament itself where team success is prioritized and your individual performance is key to attaining that success. The desire to perform well for the team adds importance to each shot and can put additional pressure on the golfer. Regardless of the reason, the vast majority of golfers feel pressure at some point during their competitive career, and their response to that pressure significantly impacts their ability to perform.

Everyone handles pressure in their own way and you'll have to develop your own method as you progress through life. Personally, I used a three-part system to overcome pressure and play my best in big events. First, my general perspective on life is very positive. I'm grateful for opportunities to learn, compete and progress each and every day. I understand every situation in life is a learning experience and regardless of the outcome, I cannot fail if I give 100% effort and learn from my mistakes (and victories). Sure, short-term outcomes may not always turn out how I imagined and that can be frustrating, but evolving as a golfer and person requires *extreme perseverance*. This outlook allows me to approach pressure situations with the understanding that I don't have to be perfect. It's ok to make a mistake, as long as I did everything in my power to achieve success, learned from the mistake, and returned to fight another day. The process of performing under pressure, learning from mistakes and sharpening your skills based on ruthless self-evaluation is exactly what leads to growth and development as a golfer. I seek out these situations as often as possible.

Second, regardless of the situation, I work my tail off to make sure I'm prepared for it. It could be a golf tournament, job interview, coaching engagement or anything else for that matter. The recipe for success is always the same; *relentless preparation.* This cannot be understated, in fact, I believe preparation is the key remedy for pressure. If you've done everything in your power to prepare for an event, you have nothing to worry about. Sure, you may feel common nerves on the first tee but they quickly fade away as you implement the skills you've worked on for the weeks and months leading up to the event.

Third, physically overcoming the effects of pressure. People experience pressure many different ways including shaky hands, rapid breathing, sweating, fear, and other symptoms that aren't conducive to calm, clear decision making and fluid golf swings. Many methods exist to manage physical manifestations of pressure and we won't cover them all here, but one that always works for me is deep nasal breathing. You can research the various techniques of deep breathing and test them for yourself, but the idea is slowing your heart rate back to your baseline (tournament) level. Keep in mind, tournament golf *should* elevate heart rate and alertness above baseline. Part of the reason some people perform better in tournaments is this heightened state of awareness promoting extreme focus and ability. It's all about finding a balance between heightened physical and mental awareness and calming your mind to execute golf shots. For me, deep breathing bridges those variables better than any method I've tried. Don't be afraid to research and implement different stress management tools if you struggle with pressure. There's no better place to test these methods than your next tournament or team qualifying event.

* * *

I mentioned before, I've witnessed many different ways to succeed on the golf course. It's for this reason I believe *extreme ownership* of your game is critically important for the tournament mindset. Preparing for a tournament not only means refining your mental and physical skills, but also creating a system for how you operate on the golf course. Not just any system either, one tailored to *your* specific skillset highlighting your strengths, minimizing weaknesses and eliminating distractions. In my experience, the best players executing a refined system operate with confidence and purpose, which in turn leads to calm, decisive actions on the course. In fact, these players often appear casual or effortless as they systematically take apart the golf course. Developing this type of system requires intense preparation and self-scrutiny over time. The process of creating, testing, analyzing and adjusting your system is a long term challenge, and one that very few see to the end. When building a system, ask yourself the following questions; how would you describe your game to a stranger? Are you keenly aware of your strengths and weaknesses? Do you have course management skills tailored specifically to your game? Do you have "go to" shots for the most important moments during the round (including short-game)? Do you have unwavering confidence in your ability, allowing you to implement your system under pressure situations? Consider writing a detailed description of how you see yourself playing your best golf based on your skills. I'm not talking about creating a wishlist where you "want more distance off the tee" or "a better short-game." Sure you can work on improving those areas but I'm talking about the here and now. If you had to play the most important round of your life *tomorrow*, what would your strategy be? What skills do you possess allowing for great tournament play? Think about it this way, if I asked 10 random PGA Tour players these same questions I'm sure I'd get 10 different answers. Do you think Jordan Speith and Bryson Dechambeau share the same approach to tournament golf? *I think not*. Professional golfers are ultra committed to their style of play and very rarely venture outside their skillset during competition. Can you say the same for yourself? This entire process is meant to uncover the key component of the tournament mindset; *clarity*. Clarity about your game inspires confidence and belief in your system, and once you believe in your system you're able to make decisions and execute golf shots with conviction. This combination of clarity, confidence and conviction is the ultimate weapon for tournament golf. It's precisely the reason less talented golfers routinely beat "more talented" competition. Simply put, implementing a system highlighting your strengths while minimizing mistakes can easily overcome golfers who rely on talent alone. Remember, playing great tournament golf is a combination of scoring *and* managing risk to eliminate mistakes. I've witnessed many ultra talented golfers lose to less talented competition because of unnecessary risk taking, leading to bad course management and penalty shots. In my experience the combination of talent, extreme ownership of your game, and disciplined adherence to a system is what makes the best tournaments golfers. This conversation about owning your game and developing a system is in the "tournament mindset" section because it's a mental challenge above all else. As a competitive golfer you'll face demanding scenarios and distracting moments throughout your career, and it's your system and ability to manage expectations that determine success in the long run.

Tournament Expectations

Managing tournament expectations and eliminating distractions is a unique skill, one that comes with experience over time. I can't help you with experience, but I can explain some common pitfalls I've seen over the years and how to prepare for them in advance. Everyone views tournament golf in their own way so let me explain my approach, then go over some of things I've seen that aren't conducive to great tournament play.

My tournament expectations are very simple; prepare as well as I can, implement my system one shot at time for the duration of the event, then do a systematic evaluation of my performance in search of strengths and weaknesses. It's really that simple. Let's focus on the evaluation because everyone has their own style of golf, and I won't bore you with mine. The most important aspect of the evaluation is judging how I implemented my system in the first place. For example, was I *fully committed* on every shot during the event, or did I lose focus due to poor play or distractions? Did I manage the golf course properly, or did I take unnecessary risks leading to poor scoring and penalty shots? Did I implement a perfect pre-shot routine for every shot, or was my process interrupted by random thoughts or actions?

If I executed these aspects to my liking, I start looking for areas where my shot making was below standard. For example, perhaps I was fully committed to a shot, executed a perfect pre-shot routine, but the result was sub-standard. I take note of these shots during the evaluation, then include them in my practice plan the following week. And I'm not necessarily talking about obvious misses like a shank or chunk. I'm talking about a scenario where maybe I hit the fairway but there are overhanging tree limbs between me and the pin, and this scenario calls for a low-cut. I commit to the shot, execute the perfect pre-shot routine and hit the ball directly into the tree branches because I haven't spent enough time preparing the low-cut for tournament play.

Once I've taken note of the obvious sub-standard shots, I look to my statistics to identify weak areas in my game. This is where a program like *Decade* comes in very handy because not only does it allow for detailed statistical analysis, it compares my numbers to other college or professional golfers so I can see how I stack up. In my experience, a detailed tournament evaluation combined with a powerful statistics program is the best recipe for improvement. So prepare your system, implement it to the best of your ability, then evaluate and improve based on your results.

My approach to tournament golf wasn't always this simple. As a younger player I was consumed with score above all else, and many college players fall into this trap as well. Don't get me wrong, score *is* the defining characteristic of tournament success, but I'm asking you to think about your expectations differently. I want you to think about tournaments as an opportunity to implement your system shot by shot, without emotion or awareness of score. And why is this so important? Because tournament golf can be chaotic, unpredictable and very distracting. Think about it, how many times have you witnessed players fall apart due to bad weather, bad playing partners, bad course conditions or anything else for that matter. Maybe that player is you? Do *you* expect perfect weather and course conditions? Do you expect respectful playing partners who share your enthusiasm for course etiquette and rules? Do you expect perfect shot making from start to finish? I hate to sound pessimistic, but the reality you'll soon face is that none of these variables are guaranteed to turn out how you want them in tournament golf. *In fact, your success as a tournament golfer depends on your ability to operate in crisis.* Can you play well in cold, wet conditions? Can you overcome bad playing partners? Can you stay positive on a less than perfect golf course? Because I promise you this, someone in the field will overcome these challenges, win the tournament and continue building armor against difficult situations on the course.

One occasion stands out from my early days of coaching regarding bad weather and chaos on the course. It was early in the fall season and coming from New Mexico we were accustomed to warm, sunny conditions. Our event was in Tulsa, OK where fall weather can be very unpredictable, and sure enough the weather for our event was forecasted to be cold, windy and rainy. As predicted, the weather for our opening round of 36 holes was very challenging. All the players had rain gear and umbrellas out, coaches were scrambling with towels and gloves and the course was playing nearly impossible. To make matters worse, the rain wasn't substantial enough to delay the round so players knew they were going to be on the course all day. Not surprisingly, many players showed signs of giving up before the round even started. One such player was someone I was familiar with from another team in my conference. In fact, this player was among the highest ranked golfers in the country and routinely challenged for tournament victories. But on this particular occasion he was visibly shaken and frustrated with the conditions. When I casually asked how he was doing he responded with, "this fricken sucks, coach." Of course, I understood his predicament having grown up in northern Michigan and played in every type of weather imaginable. Up to that point in my career I had never given an opposing player advice, but I liked this kid and felt compelled to say something. So I told him, “you know the feeling you get when you’re inside warming up after a long round in the cold and rain?” He responded, “yeah, that can’t come soon enough.” “Well,” I said, “you’re going to be out here for the next 9 hours so just imagine how much better that feeling will be if you’re leading the event.” He stared at me for a few seconds and right before my eyes the lightbulb turned on. In that moment he transformed from the victim of this terrible weather, to the person who would overcome the challenge and win the event. From that point forward every time I saw him over the next 9 hours he was walking with extra pace, focused and determined on the task. And not surprisingly, this player persevered in the conditions, built a substantial lead and eventually won the event the following day. As we were packing the van after the final round, this player found me and said, “thanks for straightening me out, coach. It really wasn’t that bad out there after you said that." Even though this wasn't my player, it was extremely satisfying to watch someone evolve right before my eyes. So remember, it's just a matter of perspective and you *always* have a choice between being the victim, or being the aggressor. It's a simple choice of accepting the challenge, or succumbing to it.

When your expectations change from "I expect a perfect tournament scenario," to "I understand anything is possible and regardless of the conditions I'll do everything in my power to implement my system one shot at a time," nothing can phase you on the golf course. From your pre-tournament warmup to your post-tournament evaluation, create habits allowing you to perform at your best regardless of conditions or distractions. As your system improves, the distractions of tournament golf including pressure, fear of failure, playing partners, bad weather and everything else fade away as you systematically attack the course *your way.*

-Chapter Summary-

1. In most cases, your tournament success is directly correlated to the amount of physical and mental preparation you engage in prior to the event.

2. Less talented golfers routinely beat more talented competition because of their work ethic and commitment to their system.

3. The fundamental tournament mindset includes two components: the ability to overcome pressure and extreme ownership of your game.

4. Navigating pressure, phase one: harness the power of gratitude, cultivate a growth mindset, and demonstrate extreme perseverance. Phase two, engage in relentless preparation. Phase three, employ techniques like deep breathing to overcome the physiological effects of pressure.

5. Employ extreme ownership of your game by creating a system for how you operate on the golf course.

6. Create realistic tournament expectations based on process over results, then utilize a thorough post-round evaluation to understand the current state of your game, and provide insights for improvement.

10 ACADEMICS

I don't remember exactly when it happened, but at some point (probably in my twenties) I realized that work ethic and preparation were the two factors determining my success in any given area. Soon after that discovery, "the work" became my favorite part of the process and something I embrace willingly, regardless of the task. A great work ethic combines discipline and purposeful action, the two traits most responsible for positive change. Developing a great work ethic requires discipline in all areas of your life. You cannot simply pick and choose where you will be disciplined, for this approach infiltrates other areas of your life, eventually leading to failures.

Having coached many college golfers, I'm aware that academics isn't the number one priority for some of you. If it is, that's great! Your college experience will include events and people from both athletics and academia, preparing you for life after college regardless of your career path. However, if you're not interested in academics and the very thought of homework and studying gives you anxiety, fear not, I'm here to help.

First, let me remind you of the stark reality facing college golfers; only 1 in 16,486 male golfers achieve full-time status on the PGA Tour. So what's your plan if you're not the one that makes it? Well, you'll face reality like the other 16,485 golfers that don't make it, choosing a career path and moving on with life. Your path may include golf in some way, but it won't include playing in the Master's or the Open Championship. I know, I sound pessimistic and that's not my intent. I'm simply reminding you that most collegiate golfers end their playing career after the final round of their senior season. *That's a fact.* So think about academics as your opportunity to develop skills that translate into earnings in the event you don't become a professional golfer.

Thankfully, there's a solution to the academic challenge and you probably already know what it is. You must *dominate* the academics! That's right, let's reframe how you think about assignments, homework, testing and accountability. My first suggestion, be grateful for the opportunity to earn a college degree. Did you know less than 10% of the world's population has a four year college degree? And for some of you, you're attending college with a scholarship, meaning the school is paying for your degree! Unbelievable! This is the opportunity of a lifetime, *capitalize on it*! And here's the great news, anyone can achieve success in the classroom with the correct perspective. Once you decide academics are a top priority and you'll do everything in your power to achieve success, it's all down hill from there. Yes, you will face challenges along the way but anything worth doing is difficult, and the end result is well worth the effort.

During my years as a university student I developed a four-part academic strategy that helped me graduate with honors from both my Bachelor's, and Master's degree programs (above 3.75 GPA). First, you must introduce yourself to the professor (preferably on the first day of class), letting him/her know you're a student athlete on the golf team. This step is vital because it creates a personal connection with the professor and opens a line of communication. Trust me, you're going to need it. Student athletes miss class and require special attention from professors. And here's the truth, some professors aren't interested in giving special attention or make-up exams to student athletes they don't know or like. It's simply human nature. But if you introduce yourself and let the professor know you're there to work, it pays dividends down the road.

Second, you must read the syllabus. A syllabus is a blueprint for the class listing all assignment due dates, office hours, contact information and other important details pertaining to the class. Nothing bothers professors more than students asking questions about the class that are clearly outlined on the syllabus. Most professors in America hand out and discuss their syllabus on the first day of the semester. I would always use a new notebook or binder for each class, attaching the syllabus to the inside cover for easy access. I checked the syllabus at the beginning of each week making sure I was up to date on assignments and exam preparation. Easy.

Third, Go to class and be present.

Without question, this is the most important aspect of my strategy. It goes without saying that success in the classroom starts with being in class. But that's not enough. If you simply show up to class but are lost on social media or messaging friends, you might as well stay at home. When you're in class turn off the phone, take off your headphones and participate with the professor. I know, the subject matter may not be interesting (to you) and it's difficult to pay attention. Doesn't matter. You must focus and get what you can from the class. I promise you this, even if the subject matter isn't compelling to you, you can still learn from the professor by simply paying attention and asking questions. However, if you refuse to participate and spend class-time on the phone, you can expect a less than favorable experience with the professor. Think about it, how would you feel if you were giving a lecture and everyone in the room was on their phone? Then, halfway through the lecture someone asked you a question about material you already covered because they were on social media and not paying attention to you. I think you know the answer. Show up to class, be present, stay off your phone and interact with the professor, you'll thank me for it later.

Lastly, do the work and don't fall behind. As a student athlete I needed a strategy to stay up to date on assignments and exam preparation. There were only so many hours in the day and my athletic schedule demanded most of them. So the truth you'll soon discover is simple, you must sacrifice the remaining hours for your academic success. My schedule looked something like this; 5:30 a.m. team workouts, followed by breakfast and class from 8 a.m. - 12 p.m., a quick lunch then off to practice until 5-6 p.m., every day. Notice you don't see any time for studying on that schedule? To ensure success in the classroom I scheduled evening study in the library every day from 7 p.m. until I was finished with the day's work. It didn't matter if I had assignments due or not, I made this part of my routine to not only stay up to date, but occasionally get ahead in my classes. Ultimately, this consistent approach to getting classwork done on-time offered an unintended consequence; *freedom*. That's right, while many of my teammates were scrambling to complete assignments and studying for exams, I was free to practice longer, hang out with friends and partake in social events on campus. What I sacrificed was TV, video games, social media and other unimportant (attention grabbing) activities to stay current on academics.

Ultimately, you must create a plan prioritizing academics, communicate with professors and ask questions along the way. Also, most universities have an "academic success center" where tudors are standing by to help, regardless of the subject matter. I truly believe the only way to fail academically is by retreating from the challenge. Instead, accept the academic responsibility, create a bullet proof schedule and never give up. Not only will you achieve high marks and learn something, you'll have more time for the activities you enjoy.

A final word of caution on academics, neglecting classwork is the number one reason student athletes miss playing time. All the major interscholastic (athletic) associations in America (NCAA, NJCAA, NAIA) have academic standards that must be upheld to maintain athletic eligibility. In most cases, you're required to complete 12 credit hours per semester at a minimum 2.0 GPA. To be frank, most student athletes meet this requirement with little trouble. That said, the student athletes operating below this standard are typically doing things like missing class, falling behind on assignments and not communicating with professors. Of course, all of these variables are within your control and falling below a 2.0 GPA is (easily) avoidable if you engage in the academic process. If you do fall below the academic standard it's very likely your coach will suspend your athletic privileges until your grades improve. Personally, I'd set a team academic standard far surpassing the requirements of the athletic association. Falling below the team standard could mean a week off from playing or some extra time in the student success center. Regardless of the team you join there will be academic standards. So prioritize your studies and you'll always be available for practice and tournaments. By committing to the academic process you'll have the confidence to dominate your classes and stay on the path to achieving your goals.

-Chapter Summary-

1. Preparation and work ethic determine your success in any given area.

2. Committing to academics is your opportunity to develop skills that translate into earnings in the event you don't become a professional golfer.

3. Consider the following four-part system for excelling in academics: create a working relationship with the professor, understand and monitor the syllabus, go to class and be present, stay up to date on assignments.

11 STRENGTH & CONDITIONING

For the past twenty five years my focus and passion centered on three areas; golf, strength and conditioning and nutrition. For no particular reason my passion for fitness started in my late teens and has carried on throughout my adult life. As a teenager I read everything I could get my hands on (we still didn't have internet), joined local gyms and learned from strength and conditioning experts. My curiosity for strength and conditioning eventually led to a bachelors degree in exercise science and health promotion, and a masters degree in applied exercise science and sports performance training. Not only have I researched this area thoroughly, I've engaged in the training for the majority of my adult life. My commitment to health and fitness is the reason I can still perform (physically) like I did in my twenties, although I don't recover from exercise quite like I used to.

So why is your physical health important? Well, research clearly identifies exercise as a main contributor to overall health. Also, strength and conditioning programs are a preventative measure for almost every chronic disease we know of. Of course nutrition, lifestyle and genetics contribute to your overall health as well. So aside from maintaining your quality of life, why is strength and conditioning important for your golf career?

The answer is multifaceted. First, let's talk about strength and conditioning as it relates to competitive golf. Simply put, your strength and conditioning protocol should be aimed at optimizing your mental and physical performance. Look no further than players like Tiger Woods, Dustin Johnson, Bryson Dechambeau, Brooks Koepka and Rory McIlroy for the importance of a strength and conditioning program. These players transformed their bodies to maximize their potential on, and off the golf course.

Reaching your physical peak requires

intense, targeted workouts that progressively get harder over time. Research supports the benefits of "periodized" strength and conditioning programs on golf specific performance (clubhead speed, driving distance, etc.). A periodized strength and conditioning program targets different areas of fitness adaptation (hypertrophy, strength, power, etc.), through specific exercise design (exercise type, sets, reps, rest). These programs are designed specifically for each sport based on the unique physical requirements of the athlete and competitive season. Most universities in America employ strength and conditioning specialists implementing these types of exercise programs. Personally, I have engaged in this type of exercise and coached it for many years. The bottom line, it works. If you join a college golf program in America you can expect this type of exercise program as part of your weekly regimen.

You may be wondering how other training methods like crossfit, high intensity interval training (HIIT) or circuit training effect golf performance. Unfortunately, research regarding these specific training methods and their effect on golf performance don't currently exist (to my knowledge). However, I can tell you from personal experience that any form of training is better than none, assuming you perform exercises with correct form and don't overtrain. But we're talking about optimizing your physical ability on the golf course, and in my opinion, there's no better way than executing a comprehensive (periodized) golf specific training program, implemented by a strength and conditioning specialist. The benefits are twofold, you'll be learning from an expert and engaging in a comprehensive program targeting all areas of physical ability. For example, a comprehensive training program should include elements of the following training adaptations; anatomical adaptation, stability and balance, hypertrophy, strength, power, mobility, flexibility and cardiovascular conditioning. If your current training protocol doesn't include one or more of these areas, you're probably not optimizing your physical ability.

Improving physical characteristics like balance, stability, mobility and cardiovascular fitness can be accomplished many different ways (yoga, pilates, running, biking, etc.). However, if one of your goals is maximizing clubhead speed and distance, you will eventually need to engage in a targeted strength training program. Admittedly, there are tools and methods available to improve clubhead speed that don't include lifting weights. These tools (speed sticks, plyometrics, etc.) aim to improve your neuromuscular efficiency. In other words, these methods improve the connection between your brain, central nervous system and musculature to optimize a particular movement pattern. In this case, the golf swing. This *is* an effective way to improve your swing speed. However, once you optimize neuromuscular efficiency you no longer see (significant) improvement with continued training. If you never lifted a weight, neuromuscular training is the next best thing for speed. However, we're not looking for "the next best thing", we're looking to optimize. Therefore, if you are planning to achieve your maximum clubhead speed and distance, you'll eventually need a strength training program in conjunction with neuromuscular training. Simply put, larger, stronger muscles are capable of producing more force, and more force production leads to greater swing speed potential.

Don't get me wrong, I'm not suggesting you turn into a bodybuilder. Just use players like Tiger, Rory and Bryson as your guide. Each of these players significantly increased lean muscle mass and strength, without sacrificing flexibility or (joint) range of motion. These physical enhancements led to improved clubhead speed and overall distance. Now, I don't have each player's specific workout routine in front of me, but based on their comments about fitness and weight lifting, I can assume they're committed to a strength and conditioning protocol.

Ok that's all well and good, but what if you've never engaged in a strength and conditioning program? Maybe you're feeling anxious about your ability in the gym and how you'll compare with your teammates and peers. This is a common apprehension among young people, especially males (because of our egos). So if you're feeling this way don't worry about it, it will eventually go away if you remember one simple rule; don't gauge your success in the gym by comparing yourself to others. In other words, there will always be someone who's bigger, faster and stronger than you. It's ok guys, you can accept this. Instead, judge your success on one fundamental question; am I creating a better version of myself today? Improving your strength and conditioning is like building a house, results don't happen overnight. In fact, progress can be painstakingly slow. Is it difficult, yes. But this is your opportunity to build a better version of yourself. How cool is that!

A productive relationship with exercise starts with your mindset. Think about exercise as a lifelong endeavor, not something you'll do because your coach requires it. The benefits of a strength and conditioning program go far beyond the physical improvement of your body. Lifting weights and training your cardiovascular system are not only physically difficult, but mentally challenging as well. In my opinion, there is no better way to prepare for, and overcome adversity than executing a difficult strength and conditioning protocol day after day. Every workout is a new challenge and when you're finished, you feel a unique sense of accomplishment and self worth.

I can say from twenty five years of experience, improving and maintaining your physical body is worth the time and effort. I am infinitely grateful to my younger self for committing to an active lifestyle. So don't worry about your age, current level of fitness or (perceived) fears about exercise. Just get started. Learn everything you can about fitness, nutrition and well-being. You won't always feel like working out, but that's the best time to get it done. When I'm facing a difficult workout or lacking motivation I simply remind myself of the process I'm committed to... *Show up, give 100%, overcome adversity, become a better version of myself today*

* * *

The majority of college golf programs in the United States have some version of mandatory team workouts. Granted, I can't speak for all coaches in America but I know plenty that implement training programs for their players. So it's a good idea to mentally prepare for team workouts. However, maybe you don't believe in physical training or don't want to wake up at 5am for team workouts. I don't necessarily agree with this perspective, but I get it. To better understand the reasoning behind team workouts, you should examine the coach's perspective.

First, why do most college golf teams have mandatory physical fitness at the brink of dawn? I think it's fairly clear, but coaches want their players in top physical condition to handle the rigors of a college golf season. Ok that's fair enough, right? But you may be asking, "can't we exercise sometime other than 6 a.m."? Well, not really. We all know daylight is required to play golf and classes typically meet during the morning hours between 8 a.m.-12 p.m. So that leaves the afternoon for practice and time on the course. The remaining (evening) hours should be dedicated to studying, homework and rest. Understandably, you might be thinking you could workout on your own at a more suitable time. Surely there's a free hour somewhere on your schedule? Yes, that may be true. You're not always busy as a student athlete. But that's not the point, the coach is counting on team workouts for benefits beyond physical fitness; team culture, bonding, and unity. These team characteristics take shape through shared struggle and for most young adults, getting up at 5:30 a.m. is a struggle on its own. Add to that a very challenging workout designed by a professional strength and conditioning coach and you've got a very demanding situation. But here's the key, you're engaging in this situation with your teammates. These are the moments when a group of individuals become teammates, and teammates become lifelong friends. These are the moments spoken about 20 years later at the team reunion. Trust me, you don't want to miss the opportunity of shared struggle with your teammates. The collective sense of accomplishment and team unity is something you’ll never forget. So embrace the physical and mental challenge of a strength and conditioning program. It's the first step to building the most powerful, confident version of yourself.

-Chapter Summary-

1. Physical exercise is a preventative measure for most, if not all chronic diseases.

2. Most modern tour players engage in a strength and conditioning protocol to optimize their physical and mental ability.

3. Building and maintaining strength and conditioning is a lifelong endeavor. Don't worry about where you are now, just start the journey and build one day at a time.

4. Embrace mandatory workouts as an opportunity to bond with teammates while building an unbreakable team culture.

12 RECRUITING

If you're already a member of a college golf program, you may want to skip ahead to the next section. However, if you're currently looking for a program or just don't know where to start, continue on.

Let's tackle the most important question first; how exactly do you join a college golf program? Unfortunately, you can't just show up on campus and declare yourself a member of the team. No, you must be recruited first and generally speaking, recruitment is a four part process.

First and foremost, coaches evaluate your current athletic and academic ability. Your athletic evaluation may include past golf tournament results, technical analysis of your fundamentals and (coaches) watching you play and practice in person. This information is used to assess and project your future ability. Simple enough. Next, coaches evaluate your high school transcripts and test scores (SAT, ACT, etc.) to determine if your academic record satisfies their university's standard. In most cases, you either meet the university academic standard, or you don't. There isn't much gray area here, so if you're planning to attend a premium academic university in America, you'll need top marks throughout high school.

Step two is a series of phone or video interviews with the coaching staff to build rapport and ensure you're a good fit with their current roster. The coaches may also interview your parents, former golf coaches and any additional references you provide. This is an underrated part of the process and one you should take seriously. If the coach doesn't think you'll mesh with their current roster you could miss your opportunity. When interviewed, give thoughtful, honest answers and have some questions of your own prepared for the coaches. Researching the school, facilities and history of the golf team shows you're interested in their program and willing to go the extra mile. Believe me, this small amount of work goes a long way with the coaching staff.

Third, a campus visit. Coaches want you

to see their campus and facilities in person before you commit to their program. Of course, not everyone gets offered a campus visit and some recruits simply cannot make the trip (international students, bad timing, etc.). Not to worry, this step isn't required and most universities do a good job displaying athletic (and academic) facilities on their website and social media page(s). However, if you're offered a campus visit and you can manage the logistics, you should absolutely take it. College will be your home away from home for the next four years, make sure you feel comfortable with the housing options, campus, golf facilities and surrounding area.

The final step is the offer. If you get to this stage you've satisfied the coach's criteria for athletic and academic ability, and now it's a matter of finances. Please understand, coaches don't have unlimited scholarship money in their budget. In fact, universities competing within NCAA guidelines only have approximately four (full) scholarships to divide amongst their roster. Collegiate rosters typically have 8-12 players, so not everyone receives a full athletic scholarship. Quite the opposite actually. Most scholarship offers contain both athletic, and academic money. Of course, qualifying for an academic scholarship means you have the requisite high school grades and placement test scores (SAT, ACT). If you *do* receive an offer from a coach, it arrives in the form of a "national letter of intent" (NLI) and "grant in aid" (GIA) form. The NLI is a binding agreement between you and the college stating your intent to play for the school, and the GIA is your scholarship offer. Also, your NLI and GIA are year to year agreements, so you'll have to sign new paperwork for each of your 4-5 years at college. Make sure you discuss this entire process with your coach *prior* to signing any papers.

The next question, how do you get noticed by coaches in the first place? The short answer, play. *Play a lot.* Make no mistake, coaches need tournament results to gauge your ability. Therefore, if you live in America and aspire to play college golf you should do everything in your power to join your high school golf team. In most cases, high school coaches are connected with college coaches and can help with your recruitment. This connection is invaluable if you're not one of the best amateur players in your age group and need help getting noticed. Also, high school golf is like a dress rehearsal for college golf. You will learn how to interact with teammates and coaches, play against good amateur competition, all while managing academics and social events. Of course, many high schools have limited roster positions and you'll have to compete for your spot on the team. I know from experience these tryouts can be highly competitive and a position on the team isn't guaranteed. Make sure you're prepared when your opportunity comes because making the high school golf team significantly improves your chances of playing college golf.

Of course, just playing high school golf isn't enough to be recruited by a major university. In fact, the top college golf programs typically recruit three to four years into the future. This means you should be playing every amateur event you can, as early as you can. Personally, I started playing junior golf tournaments before age 10, and I know it’s possible to start even younger now.

So, perhaps you're wondering which amateur events, aside from high school, give you the best chance at being noticed by a college coach. Well, if you live in America you have many options. First, I recommend trying to qualify for the major (national) amateur tournaments. Examples of these events in the United States are the U.S. Amateur, the Western Amateur and the Junior World Championship, among others. The major amateur events typically have handicap restrictions and require local and regional qualifying to gain entry. However, qualifying and performing well in major amateur competition goes a long way with college coaches. If you don't live in the United States, research and identify the most prestigious amateur events in your country and make a plan to compete in them. Coaches in America pay close attention to the major international events, and in some cases, attend these events in person to watch the top players.

If you can't participate in the big amateur events that's ok, there are other ways of getting noticed. For example, in the U.S. we have the American Junior Golf Association (AJGA), which basically serves as a national mini-tour for amateur golfers. Players earn ranking points based on tournament results, and those rankings are displayed on the AJGA website. Coaches pay close attention to the rankings. The AJGA is available for boys and girls of all ages (12-19), from anywhere in the world.

Admittedly, playing AJGA events can be expensive, but if you *can* play, you'll have access to world class amateur competition on some of the best courses in America. In fact, you may have heard of some former AJGA players of the year; Tiger Woods, Paula Creamer, Phil Mickelson, Cristie Kerr and Jordan Speith to name a few. If your country has a national amateur golf association like this, take advantage of everything they have to offer. In some cases, they have access to college coaches and resources for recruiting in addition to their tournament schedule.

If you cannot play the national events or travel to distant tournaments, you still have options. For example, most states in America have amateur golf associations and in some cases, more than one per state. These associations host tournaments and teaching clinics within each (respective) state, making travel much more affordable and convenient. So don't worry if you're not playing the biggest amateur events in the country, stay focused on building a resume and improving your game. Playing locally can help with both, and you'll gain valuable experience in the process.

If you're not from the United States it's a little tougher to get recruited, but still very possible. First, play as many national events as you can, then fill in your resume with quality events in your area. You may be wondering how to determine if the events you're playing in are "quality". In my opinion, your *best* resource for finding quality tournaments is the World Amateur Golf Ranking (WAGR) website. If you don't know about WAGR, now is a good time to learn. Simply put, WAGR is the premier amateur ranking association in the world, and college coaches are keenly aware of the top players. However, simply participating in a WAGR event doesn't guarantee you'll appear on their world ranking. To appear on the world ranking you need a quality finish in one of their events (typically top 10 or better). Once you've made the list, you'll earn points for each subsequent tournament you participate in.

For more information about WAGR

simply visit their home page (wagr.com) and you'll have access to the latest amateur golf rankings, past and future events near you, and much more. For you international players, WAGR is one of the best ways to get noticed by American coaches so prioritize and register for as many WAGR events as you can.

If you do everything I just outlined there's a very good chance you'll get recruited. However, every year many deserving players go unnoticed and don't find a college program to join. As an insurance policy you may consider a recruiting agency to help you through the process (especially international players). Each recruiting agency is different, but in most cases they will create an online profile for you including your playing resume, swing videos and academic history. Then the recruiting agency contacts coaches on your behalf, sending the online profile for review. If the coach is interested he or she will contact you directly to continue the recruiting process.

Of course, these agencies aren't free. But if you're struggling to find a school, your chances of being recruited significantly improve by working with a top recruiting agency. If you're wondering which agency to work with, simply ask (each agency) where they've placed athletes in the past. The bigger agencies have a long history of placing student athletes at high quality universities. Don't settle for anything less.

Finally, go ahead and contact coaches directly if you think that's your best option. But first, a word of caution. Don't contact a coach via email without including your resume. Like I said before, coaches want to see your playing history and high quality swing videos presented in a professional manner. If you simply email a coach letting them know you're available and ready to play for their team, your chances of getting recruited are slim to none. The top programs receive hundreds of emails per year from players around the world. Make sure you stand out by preparing a clean, thorough playing resume and quality swing videos that include various golf shots and camera angles. Additionally, write a thoughtful note describing why you should have a roster position on their team. Remember, professional golf coaches earn a living through the success of their team so they're only looking for the best possible candidates for their roster. If you want to be considered, do everything in your power to create a quality presentation of yourself.

-Chapter Summary-

1. In basic terms, your recruitment is a three-part process. Initially, coaches evaluate your playing resume and current skills on the course. Next, they take into account your high school transcripts and major test scores. Finally, you participate in meetings and interviews with coaches to gauge your compatibility with the team and establish mutual understanding about the program.

2. Your best opportunity to get noticed by college coaches is playing as many high-level tournaments as you can.

3. If you're struggling with recruitment go ahead and contact coaches directly. Be sure to present yourself in a professional manner. Include your playing resume, current swing videos, a brief biography of yourself, and relevant references if you have them.

13 THE COACH

I grew up in the sports culture of America. At an early age I participated in junior golf, baseball, flag football, soccer and just about every other sport you can think of. Not surprisingly, there was always a coach demonstrating fundamentals, teaching sportsmanship and preparing us to win. In most cases the coach was revered, almost above reproach. As players, we understood the coach was in charge. We did what was asked, worked hard and accepted the discipline if we failed to achieve the team standard. In case you're wondering, back in my day "discipline" took the form of extra drills, physical conditioning or time off the field. The coach had final say on everything, and for the most part, everyone accepted it.

So why am I telling you this? Well, not everyone playing college golf in America is from the United States, and other cultures may have very different relationships with their coaches. My goal with this section is explaining the player/coach relationship as it pertains to college golf in America, and providing some information to navigate difficult times should they arise.

Joining a college golf program means you're entering a unique relationship with a coach, and for better or worse, this coach significantly impacts the next 4-5 years of your life (or more). Understanding this relationship is imperative for your success as a student athlete. I certainly can't speak for other coaches, but I can explain the expectations I had for student athletes joining my team. I could probably write an entire book on this subject, but let's stick to the three fundamental characteristics I looked for in new student athletes.

Number one, effort. I often told my players that it doesn't matter how you perform on the course, the classroom or in the gym, as long as you're giving 100% effort in all areas. Don't get me wrong I'm very competitive and I love winning, but occasionally the competition gets the best of you or you have a bad day. Believe me, I (and other coaches) understand the pressure you're under and the challenges you face every day. What I'm looking for is a person who responds to the challenge with great effort, day after day. Simple.

Number two, be accountable. In chapter four I discussed accountability and how it relates to your success. It's very important that you consider this information and make a real effort to be responsible for all aspects of your life. I love coaching college golfers. What I don't love is continually reminding players to finish homework assignments, show up on time for practice or maintain the behavioral standards set forth by the college. I certainly didn't expect perfection, but I did expect players to be accountable for their life on campus. For example, you should know the expectations for practice, workouts, academics, behavioral standards and consequences for non-compliance. Remember, there will be team and university standards you must uphold, and falling below these standards could mean disciplinary action. Most universities have drug and alcohol programs that implement random testing throughout the year. Should you test positive for an illegal drug you could face an athletic suspension (penalties vary among schools), and whatever team discipline your coach deems necessary. How about academics? Yes it's true, you are held to a higher standard than traditional university students. Falling below the university or team academic standard may require suspension of athletic privileges. Keep in mind, you are now working with a professional coach, and he/she has clear expectations for you. You are expected to work hard, uphold team and university standards *and* perform well athletically. You are choosing to join a college golf program, upholding your end of the bargain is part of the deal. So be accountable for your life on campus and you'll earn the respect of your coaches.

Number three, be coachable. Remember, when you join a college golf program the coach is (on some level) trusting you with his/her career. Now, I'm not saying the coach's job is in your hands, but the team is a reflection of the coach, and your success or failure matters. Part of my job as a coach was sharing past experiences and knowledge so players could avoid common mistakes. We as coaches want you to be successful. I'm not asking you to blindly follow someone's lead, especially if you have moral or ethical disagreements. I'm suggesting you be open minded, listen, experiment with new ideas and approach each situation with curiosity. Personally, I wanted my players to discover answers on their own. I provided guidance and leadership based on my experience, but I tried not to force my perspective as the only way forward. That being said, if a coach adamantly wants you to implement change in a certain area there's probably a good reason. Open your mind, listen, learn and let your coach help you reach your full potential.

Ok so you're giving great effort, accountable for all aspects of your life on campus and highly coachable. Perhaps you're wondering what you should you expect from the coach in return? This is a great question and it's important to have expectations of your own. Every coach is different, but the great ones I know share common traits. For example, all great coaches care about their players success, both on and off the course. They are invested in your future and truly want what's best for you. Also, they are fully engaged in *your* process of becoming great. They are with you at 5 a.m. workouts, afternoon practices, study hall, tournaments and are always available for a chat (about anything). They research the game, stay current on equipment and search for innovative practice methods to develop and sharpen your skills. In short, they are fully committed to your success.

So when you're searching for a college golf program and coach, keep these characteristics in mind. Before you sign with a coach ask questions about their involvement in your process (golf, academics, strength & conditioning, etc). If you're speaking with a coach and it doesn't feel right, that's ok, it probably isn't a good fit. Keep searching and find a coach that's excited about the process and shares your vision for success. Remember, this is a serious commitment so gather as much information about the coach and program as you can before signing.

Here's a pro tip, the best tool for gathering real information about the coach and program is speaking with current and former players from that program. Don't be afraid to ask a coach during the recruiting process to put you in contact with his players.

As a coach I offered this to all potential recruits. I wanted the recruit to understand what they were committing to from a player's perspective, and I asked my current players (who they were speaking with) to be completely honest about their experience with me and the program in general. You can't always take the information as gospel, but if you speak to enough players you'll gain valuable insight regarding the experience at that school, and how the coach interacts with the team.

Now, there *are* situations where a player simply cannot get along with the coach and the relationship turns toxic. In this situation the player has several options including a transfer, but I'd ask the player a few questions before exercising that option. First, is the player doing everything the coach asks? For example, is he a good teammate? Is he on-time for team meetings? Does he attend class and work hard during practice? These are basic requirements of all teams, and poor performance in any of these areas could lead to friction between player and coach.

The next question I'd ask is about communication. How often does the player speak with the coach one on one? If he has an issue (academic, athletic or otherwise), does he express that to the coach? I recommend building a personal relationship with the coach as soon as possible so you're able to have difficult discussions without compromising the relationship. This is a 4-5 year commitment and there will be occasions where you don't necessarily agree with the coach. Make sure the relationship is strong enough to endure a tough conversation or two.

Ok let's assume this player is a great teammate and does his best to communicate with the coach. If he's still having problems there are two potential options. First, the player honors the commitment to the school and stays with the team. In this scenario the player maintains the highest standards for himself, relying on teammates for support and guidance throughout the semester. In my experience this is the option most players choose because they want to remain loyal to their teammates and follow through on their commitment to the school. The second option is transferring to another school, assuming the player wants to continue with college golf. The rules for transferring change year to year so I won't cover them here. But you should know it's possible to transfer if you're struggling with the team or coach. If the relationship is simply too toxic to maintain, schedule a meeting with the athletic director and discuss your options.

-Chapter Summary-

1. Your college coach will significantly impact the next 4-5 years of your life.

2. As a coach, I looked for three main attributes from my players: effort, accountability and coachability.

3. Interview potential coaches and make sure their expectations align with yours. Ask questions about the coach's involvement with practice, tournament evaluations, strength and conditioning, academics, and anything else you think is relevant to your development as a player and person.

14 FINAL THOUGHTS

Your success as a college golfer depends on your ability to manage all aspects of life on campus. I hope the material in this book helps define the college experience, providing tools to help you along the way. There's plenty to think about and you may be wondering how to put it all together. It starts with a commitment. A commitment that you'll do everything in your power to achieve success in all areas of your life. And your perspective on this commitment is key. Don't feel pressure to perfect everything at once. Instead, focus on incremental improvements day after day leading to a more efficient process, on and off the course. Don't worry about outside pressure, judgement or someone else's idea of success. Don't compare yourself with others or try to live up to someone else's standards.

This is your journey, define your version of success and create a plan to achieve it.

Never forget why you're in college in the first place; *to chase your dreams.* If you aspire to play professional golf, that's great. If you don't intend on pursuing a career in golf after you graduate, that's great too. Either way, use this opportunity in college to create an unstoppable work ethic that serves you for the rest of your life. And don't forget to have fun while you're at it! If you're pursuing a difficult goal there will be challenging moments ahead, make sure to stay present and enjoy the process along the way.

Remember, achieving greatness always requires some level of risk. Don't shy away from risk, *prepare for it.* French biologist Louis Pasteur once said, "chance favors only the prepared mind". Make no mistake, you may only get *one* chance at accomplishing your dream. Treat every day as if it were the most important day of your life. Read another book, do another workout, practice another hour. Nothing is guaranteed in this life, but *chance favors the prepared mind.*

Above all else, do not let anyone or anything get in the way of your goals.

People get uncomfortable when you declare lofty goals and pursue them aggressively. You may hear your dream is unattainable and unrealistic, but these people are just projecting their own fears and doubts on you. Don't listen. Simply smile, thank them for their concern and go about your business knowing you're doing what's right for you. Because the truth is, *your goal is attainable, you simply need to claim it.* Yes, your goals may require incredible discipline and sacrifice, but that's the cost of all worthy endeavors. Embrace the journey and give it everything you've got.

My final suggestion, be humble in your approach to life. In my experience, humility is the most attractive personality trait. Being a great teammate requires humility, hard work, accountability, and willingness to help others. If you're generous with your time and knowledge, I promise you'll feel a sense of value and self worth bringing new understanding to life itself. When you help someone achieve their goals, they return the favor twofold. This type of environment accelerates learning and skill development, pushing you further than you ever thought possible. So take advantage of this amazing opportunity to grow and thrive as a college golfer, *it's the greatest time of your life.*

ABOUT THE AUTHOR

James Berry

James Berry is a high performance coach from the United States with over a decade of experience working with college golfers. His expertise doesn't stop at the tee; Berry also guides individuals towards success through the power of mindset and lifestyle transformations.

Coach Berry spent the majority of his youth and early adulthood pursuing excellence in competitive golf. He won a high school state championship with his teammates in Michigan, then became a decorated NCAA collegiate golfer, continuing on to professional golf after graduation. James eventually made his way to New Mexico Junior College where he coached a very competitive golf program for 7 seasons.

Coach Berry also has passion for strength and conditioning. He holds a Bachelor's degree in exercise science and health promotion, along with a Master's degree in applied exercise science and sports performance training. James has worked with hundreds of collegiate athletes from various sports to create and implement specialized strength and conditioning protocols. He is an ardent supporter of physical education, nutrition and healthy lifestyle.

Coach Berry's roots in competitive golf inspired him to pursue and develop the foundational elements of mindset training. Over two decades, he has honed his personal mindset mantra, emphasizing discipline, accountability, resilience, and confidence. These principles have not only served him well but have also been key drivers of success for his college golf teams. At the end of the day, Berry's mental strategy isn't exclusive to athletes; it's a master plan designed to empower anyone to conquer goals, whether they're on the fairway or navigating life's many challenges.

REFERENCES

Fitts, P. M., & Posner, M. I. (1967). Human performance. Oxford, England: Brooks/Cole.

M. (2020, October 26). What Are the Odds Of Becoming a Professional Golfer? - Club And Tee. Club and Tee. https://clubandtee.com/odds-of-becoming-a-professional-golfer/.

College Golf By the Numbers - High School Golf. (2021, March 2). High School Golf. https://www.highschoolgolf.org/college-golf-by-the-numbers/.

Printed in Great Britain
by Amazon

53632586R00106